DIVINE SECRETS
OF AFFLUENT
WOMEN

DIVINE SECRETS OF AFFLUENT WOMEN

THE GUIDE TO OWNING YOUR WEALTH

KIENA LEE

NEW DEGREE PRESS

DIVINE SECRETS OF AFFLUENT WOMEN
The Guide To Owning Your Wealth

ISBN   978-1-64137-980-9   *Paperback*

           978-1-64137-867-3   *Kindle Ebook*

           978-1-64137-868-0   *Ebook*

DEDICATION

This book is dedicated to women around the world who have been assaulted by their husband or boyfriend. You are my Heroines. Each and every day, I pray for you and dream of the day when you become financially fearless and free from violence.

CONTENTS

———

APPENDICES

PROLOGUE

———

"I'm not good at math!"

Maybe you've said it or heard it before, but negative self-talk like this keeps you from achieving financial success. No one is born a numbers person. Women are born with the ability to do math. Getting the wrong answer in calculations does not mean that we are not genetically predisposed to be financial geniuses. Our problem solving or finance skills can improve with hard work and practice.

So many women today are hesitant to be accountable for money or think about wealth, which is detrimental to our financial stability. We find ways to avoid dealing with money. We are in debt with little savings and have no idea where our money is going. Our ignorance keeps us in a cycle of escalating poverty and debt.

At a young age, we are taught to be careful about money. Girls are taught to track spending, cut coupons, and save money while boys are taught to invest their money. As a result, women tend to leave seventy-one percent of our money in cash[1] (which is low risk and low reward) instead of investing in the stock market. Or when they do invest, women are inclined to do so much later than men.

Not only do women live longer than men, but we also tend to be the primary family caregiver, spending multiple years taking care of elderly parents and children. In all likelihood, we have fewer earning years in the workforce, thus less time to build a nest egg and to save for retirement. At some stage in our lives, every woman will have the sole responsibility for her financial future.

Our society tells us lies that women are not good with money and that women are not good at math; therefore, we need to outsource handling money to our spouse and partners. As a result, our fate is undeniably tied because we have relinquished financial control to someone else.

The truth is that these lies hold us back from financial independence. If we want to get ahead financially, retire comfortably, and stop worrying about money, we need to take back control of our finances.

Unlike the women of her generation, I watched my mom take charge of her destiny.

When I was eight years old, my mom walked out on a failed marriage, left her home in Hong Kong, and took me and my three siblings—all of us under the age of ten—to a foreign

---

1   Maya Salam, "Money Is Not Just For Men," Her Words, *New York Times*, June 14, 2019.

country. She did not know anyone in the country, and she spoke very little English. Unfortunately, she took our family's life savings and invested the money with men she didn't know and on products that she did not understand. These men swindled all her money away, and my mother became a penniless single parent with four children to support.

I admired my mother's courage and her financial independence to make her own decisions. She didn't attend formal secondary school because her parents didn't have the money. Yet, she has never been afraid to take risks.

I couldn't protect my mom from losing her wealth, but I can help other women avoid the same mistakes. So, I earned a bachelor's degree in economics and a Juris Doctorate in law from top universities and became an attorney. Early on in my career, I practiced family law—helping women obtain their fair share of the marital estate and fight for custody of their children. But something was missing. No matter how much money my clients acquired, it didn't last.

I wanted to know why.

I sought out successful self-made affluent women who are financially independent and in charge of their own destiny because I realized they thought differently about wealth. I wanted to understand what and how women, like Indra Nooyi—the former CEO of PepsiCo—and hundreds of others did differently, and how I could apply their strategies to help more women build their wealth.

Indra Nooyi

Indra wasn't born wealthy. But she did find a way to build wealth. She came to America at the age of twenty-three with only $50 in her pocket to attend graduate school in business administration. Forty years later, in 2018, she has a net worth of $80 million. She has also been listed at #1 on *Fortune* magazine's list of Most Powerful Women in Business from 2006 to 2010.

Yet despite her tremendous achievement as the highest-ranking Indian-born woman in corporate America, Indra's mom kept her grounded. In September of 2006, Indra rushed home to share the news that she had been appointed the president of PepsiCo, an iconic American company. Yet her mother refused to listen and ordered her to go and buy milk from the store. As a dutiful daughter, Indra brought the milk back. When she demanded to know why she had to buy the milk and not somebody else, her mother explained, "You might be the president of PepsiCo, and you might be on the board of directors, but when you enter this house, you're the wife, you're the daughter, and you're the mother. Nobody else can take that place. So, leave that damn crown in the garage. And don't bring it into the house." Indra's mom reminds us that even though we can afford to hire help to run errands, do the cooking and cleaning for our household, no matter how affluent we become, culturally, we still hold ourselves accountable as mother to our children, wife to our husband, and daughter to our parents.

Can self-made affluent women have it all? What makes them different than countless other women in America? Is it luck, strategy, or a combination of both? Is their wealth due to their intellectual prowess or can less-gifted women achieve this too?

What I learned has changed my hope for the future of women.

I believe that women are born to prosper. Building wealth is a strategy and skill. You have to cultivate the path to financial wealth intentionally. Once you develop a wealthy mindset and follow the principles self-made affluent women use, you too will learn to be prosperous. No matter where you are in your life journey, you can build and rebuild your financial future now.

Many lessons learned by the women featured in this book didn't come easy. It doesn't matter if you are "afraid" of money, if you're a woman in your twenties starting your adult-life, in your thirties going through transitions, in your forties balancing income across savings and spending, or in your fifties planning for your financial future, my hope is to pass these lessons and strategies along to ensure a stable financial future.*

My aim in writing this book is to show you strategies and not logistics. Without knowing your situation, I can only give you checklists and general information but not financial or legal advice. You should always consult an attorney and/ or a certified financial planner for official guidance. I truly believe that these time-tested strategies will bring you closer to financial independence. Together, we will create a world where women are financially fearless.

*Disclaimer: All content in this book is for informational purposes only; you should not construe any such information or other material as legal, tax, investment, financial, or other advice. All content is information of a general nature and does not address the circumstances of any particular individual or entity. Nothing in this book constitutes a complete statement of the matters discussed or the law relating thereto. You alone assume the sole responsibility of evaluating the merits and risks associated with the use of any information or other content in the book before making any decisions based on such information or other content. In exchange for reading the book, you agree not to hold the author, her affiliates, or any third-party service provider liable for any possible claim for damages arising from any decision you make based on information or other content made available to you through the book.

PART I

THE BEGINNING

CHAPTER 1

POWER STRUGGLE

———

The most common way people give up their power is by thinking they don't have any.

—ALICE WALKER, AUTHOR OF THE COLOR PURPLE

Money is power. For some of you, it may seem off-putting. Yet, it is an undeniable truth that with wealth, people obtain influence and respect easily.

Many women today are conditioned not to be strong, assertive, outspoken, or powerful. Our society has taught us how to dress, behave, and present ourselves. We are expected to be polite, accommodating, accepting, and nurturing. Since the evolution of hunter-gatherer societies, we are expected to take care of the children, cook, and clean the house, with the assumption that we will be economically dependent on men. Unfortunately, these expectations impact how we perceive ourselves and how we resist being fully independent adults.

Naturally, successful women intimidate us. Powerful women are thought to be threatening, overwhelming, abnormal, and unattractive. So, we cling to the perception of being power-less because female success scares men away. We avoid being financially successful as a trade-off to be in a relationship or have a family. If we make more money than men, we don't talk about it. We limit our power by ignoring, mishandling, or neglecting our money. The avoidance of power becomes our means for survival.

To make matters worse, women have complicated feelings about money. We make excuses such as:

Finance doesn't interest us. It's boring.

We feel more womanly by letting our father or husband worry about money.

We're good at making money, but someone else should take care of it.

We are artists. Money is not important. It's too time consuming and overwhelming; we have no time to learn about investing. We don't understand the financial jargon.

Throughout history, women have never been financially equal to men. Even in modern times, banks and lenders still discriminate against women. Up until 1975, women were still not allowed to open bank accounts or credit cards in their own names without a male cosigner. Even if a woman made more money than her husband or father, she still needed their signature to open an account. As a result, we are conditioned to seek male approval on financial matters, and over time, we are conflicted and afraid to change this behavior.

Gigi, Tool Shop Owner

From the age of eleven, Gigi was around her father's work as a toolmaker. He would work during the day for a tool company and, in the evenings, run his own tool and die set business in the cellar of their home. When neighbors complained about the noise, he built a tool shop and established his business. After Gigi completed high school and had a few years of experience working for a bank and insurance company, her father invited her to work in the family tool shop. She received a good salary but was not given responsibilities because her father saw her as his little girl who was incapable of handling the business.

Six years later, she married an engineer, and her father brought her husband into the family business because he fit into their business model. Gigi's father treated her differently after having her husband as an ally at work. She became an equal partner with her husband. Gigi continued running the company while raising four children. Eventually, she expanded the business and bought the shop from her father. At its peak, she had forty employees working for her. Gigi ran the tool shop for fifty years before selling it.

In her words:

> "It was the best move I ever made because if it wasn't for my husband, I probably wouldn't have gotten anywhere in the business."

Gigi couldn't get a business loan without having her husband as a co-signer forty years ago. So, she never borrowed any money. She owned and managed the only woman-owned tool shop in the 1970s. She is a pioneer businesswoman who had to challenge her own father's outdated mentality that a woman couldn't handle the business of running a male-dominated tool shop successfully while also raising children.

Today, women control half of the wealth in the United States. But why is it that many of us still lack confidence when it comes to understanding finances?

Is it because men make money, and women spend it?

Or is it because women are bad at managing finances?

Or is it because women don't have as much confidence in their careers as men do?

Or is it because talking about money is "unladylike?"

We know that none of these limiting beliefs are true. What is true, however, is that more women are the primary breadwinners in their family today. Affluent women are frugal, thus better at managing money. When we save more and spend less, we have more money set aside for retirement or to invest. We care about having a career or a calling and living a holistic family life. We are confident in discussing money and investing with a financial professional on our own. We dare to take calculated economic risks. We accept and embrace the fact that gaining power may make us less attractive to men. We believe that building a sizable fortune gives us choices and improves our circumstances.

Financial success for women is about shifting our mindset and seizing our ascension to power. It is about permitting ourselves to prosper, to wield power, to be financially responsible, and economically independent. Our financial well-being is dependent on our relationship with money. When we see money as a tool to create a meaningful life, building wealth is a natural consequence.

Is changing our mindset on wealth something everyone is capable of? Yes.

Everyone is capable of releasing old beliefs, assumptions, and conditioning about money, regardless of circumstance. Once we are aware of our thoughts and beliefs that shape our thinking and habits, we can decide to keep some or drop others. How we view the world impacts how we react to people and challenges. When we see the world as a land of opportunity, people become our allies to help achieve our goals. In the same way, if we see money as the root of all evil, we spend all our money and avoid managing it. When we perceive money as a tool, this simple mindset shift changes the way we live. We can create our own opportunities, and if we push ourselves, we can and must accept responsibility and accountability for our wealth.

Our difficulties with money are related to our fear or ambivalence about power. Affluent women view money and power as a means to an end. Building wealth is eighty percent mindset and twenty percent strategy. We are born to prosper. Making money is part of our DNA as caretakers. Embrace it.

CHAPTER 2

BORN TO PROSPER

———

So, what is holding you back from being wealthy?

Is it because you're not good with money?

Or is it because you don't have a college degree?

Lack of education or credentials should not hold you back. Financial success is possible in any field and any business. Yet our minds have been conditioned to respond negatively to cues concerning wealth-building opportunities. We struggle with our own power to make money.

Becoming wealthy is a mind game. Our state of mind and attitude determines our level of financial success. We can transform our beliefs and assumptions about what is possible no matter how difficult our circumstances or how discouraged we feel. We can acquire a wealthy mindset and learn to think like an affluent woman.

What does it take to be an affluent woman?

I had the privilege and honor to get to know some of them. Collectively, I found common traits and attributes they all have. Some of them were born with the will to persevere and the ability to overcome being raised by abusive and/or neglectful parents. They had the mindset to succeed despite their upbringing. They often overcame challenges that would destroy spirit, pride, and ambition in most people.

There is no good reason for you to think that you cannot be an affluent woman.

What we really want to do is what we are really meant to do. When we do what we are meant to do, money comes to us, doors open for us, we feel useful, and the work we do feels like play to us.

—JULIA CAMERON

Here's a portrait of the affluent women:

We focus on financial independence. We trust our own intuition and our inner diva to persevere. Some of us are well-educated but not necessarily intellectually gifted. Some of us do not have a degree. We are content because we have fulfilled our need to be self-reliant and became self-made affluent. Satisfaction comes from our families, from exceeding our goals, from helping noble causes, from work that has provided a clear path to financial independence. We have the freedom to allocate both time and money.

Integrity

Affluent women are honest with everyone. We look at things from our point of view and the point of view of others. We became rich without compromising integrity.

Independence of Thought

We think outside the box and do not follow the crowd. We are disciplined enough to search for great economic opportunities.

Work Ethnic

We work harder than most people. The harder we work, the luckier we become.

Discipline and Self-control

We prepare and plan to succeed. We are well-organized. To become wealthy, we are disciplined in thought and deed. We discipline ourselves to look forward to the future, even though most of us have overcome adversity and reversals in life.

Vocation

We see our vocation as a calling in life and not as a job.

Empathy

We get along with people and understand the backgrounds of each person. In fact, we tend to focus on the needs and interests of others, because we can't get to the next level without their help and cooperation. Once we understand the feelings of others, we are selected to lead.

Leadership Skills

We have the ability to persuade and sell our vision, our ideas, our game plan, our dreams, our product, and our services. Yet as leaders, we see beyond ourselves and perceive the true capacities and capabilities of team members. We create an environment that encourages team members to take on primary responsibility to find answers to the challenges they face. We help them see what's possible. Once they see our vision, team members take ownership of their work.

Courage to Take Financial Risks

We dare to take economic opportunities that others ignored. We are disciplined to search for great economic opportunities.

Supportive Spouse or None at All

We tend to marry someone who is positive, supportive, and brings out the best in us. As we travel along the road of life, we need someone who tends to be self-disciplined, frugal, even-tempered, secure, and accepting. Our spouse becomes an informal confidant who provides psychological support.

Frugality

We accumulate wealth by living below our means. We avoid debt at all costs. We don't want to be a burden to others.

Team of Advisors

We hire a team of trusted advisors and experts, such as CPAs, attorneys, financial planners, and investment advisors to guide us. The money we spend on valuable advice is worth its weight in gold.

Wealthy and Generous

We distribute a portion of our wealth to those in need. We have a very strong sense of community. We see the need to help others through acts of kindness. We support the noble causes—understaffed, underfunded, underappreciated, and the non-elitist. Empathy for others influences how we distribute our wealth in ways that give us great satisfaction.

We are doers who do not waste time or emotional energy complaining. We direct our energy in ways that enhance our productivity and improve our quality of life. We keep our crown hidden because we don't want to brag about our financial success. We thrive to live a balanced life by making trade-offs. We choose to be mothers, wives, and dutiful daughters who enjoy spending quality time with our families.

Truth be told…you do not need all these attributes to become affluent, but you do need to save money and live below your means. Regardless of where you are in your financial life, the good news is you can join this exclusive club of affluent women by following the tools and strategies discussed in the following chapters.

CHAPTER 3

MONEY MINDSET

"Money is simple. People make it complicated."

—JEAN CHATZKY

Do you ever wonder why affluent women are financially savvy living a balanced lifestyle while others struggle at managing money?

According to a study published by the Association for Financial Counseling and Planning Education,[2] your attitudes about money and debt are formed during your adolescence. We have a collection of thoughts and beliefs about money that shape our thoughts and habits. In fact, we can predict your financial experiences based on your parents' habits and attitudes toward money [from being financially responsible to wasteful spending].

---

2   Stephanie R. Yates, "Research Brief: Financial Socialization" *AFCPE Standard Newsletter*, 4th Quarter 2019.

How you think about money will greatly influence your financial situation. That's why it's vital to first explore what your own beliefs and opinions about money are.

Is money hard to come by?

What is money's place in your life?

If you grow up thinking that being rich is somehow wrong, you are only equipped to handle small amounts of money because your core belief is against being rich; you will spend money as quickly as you earn it.

What makes these financially savvy women different is not a "natural ability" that they were born with. They really have no clear advantage over anyone else at birth. The difference is that they've made a CHOICE to be financially savvy. They have decided to live their life the way they want and have created consistent routines that make them the way that they are. You can learn from the behavior and strategies of wealthy women and change your relationship with money.

--Mindset Challenge--

Did you know that you have a financial diva within you? Your inner diva knows intuitively how you feel about money. Let's play a game to awaken your inner financial diva.

Here's what I want you to do in the next few days (the sooner, the better):

1. Write your own money story. Begin with the relationship you want to have with money. For example, *money is my friend* or *money is good*. Making money is fun.

Open your mind and your heart. Ask yourself how does your experience with money impact the way you see yourself?

You are the creator of your own life experience. You can rewrite your story by changing your perceptions and become a better version of yourself. No situation will have meaning until you define it and give it meaning. Every day we carry hidden beliefs about money that color our perception. Inspire yourself, be open-minded, and allow your awareness to expand.

Your money story is as good as you want it to be. Although cash may be low right now, the fact is that money consistently flows in and out of your life. You have endless opportunities to generate money by using your natural gifts, talents, skills, and abilities.

You can tell a different financial abundance story and set your own standard for financial well-being. When it comes to money, there are always ups and downs. Create the money flows you desire in your story. One hidden belief around money may be that when you have money, you don't have time to enjoy spending money. Or on the flip side, when you have time, you don't have any money to spend. To reverse the thinking, your new story is "I can create both money and time to enjoy it." Tell yourself that your money is circulating, flowing, and growing.

Have fun writing your story.

2. The second thing is to create daily rituals that support your financial abundance story. One common trait all successful people have is good habits. Positive habitual routines will help you be at your best. For example, I start my day with a money mantra. When I'm getting ready in the morning, I look at myself in the mirror and use positive statements such as "Financial success is a game I play to win." Having positive beliefs about money will change your life.

If you start making these little changes, I promise you your life will never be the same again.

--Money Mind-map--

Once your inner financial diva is awakened, you're ready for the next challenge. To keep it simple, I've summarized everything in a pie chart. This is the only **Money Mind-map** you need to follow.

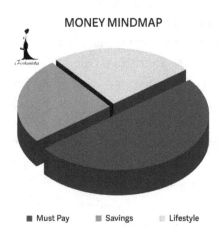

MONEY MINDMAP

■ Must Pay   ■ Savings   Lifestyle

Your income represents the entire pie. If you allocate fifty percent of your income for Must Pay expenses, twenty-five percent for Savings, and twenty-five percent for Lifestyle needs, you are one step closer to becoming financially independent. This Mind-map will help you live below your means.

Once you choose a standard of living, stick to it no matter how much your income grows. Living on seventy-five percent of your income will allow you to use the remaining twenty-five percent for your future, such as retirement, sending a child to college, or starting a business.

Use the cash method to manage lifestyle needs. To keep things simple, whatever amount remains after savings and must-pay expenses, keep it in cash.

For example: Let's say, you take home $5k per month.

1. Pay yourself first, twenty-five percent or $1,250 is for savings.
2. Fifty percent, or $2,500, is for bills that you must pay.
3. The remaining twenty-five percent or $1250—keep in cash. Allocate $250 for entertainment, $500 for shopping, and $500 for food. You can move the cash from one envelope to another, but when the cash is gone, you're done spending for the month. Simple?

That's it. A very simple system to keep track. Once you have your Money Mind-map set up, you can use it to create a detailed budget. Keep in mind that the percentage amount is not as important, as long as it doesn't go over one hundred percent. For example, you can spend thirty percent of your paycheck on things that spark joy, thirty percent for savings, and forty percent for paying bills. The key is to take control of your finances, making changes, and modifying your spending accordingly.

Saving is a key principle in our pie chart. When you make a habit of paying yourself first regularly, even in small amounts, you are well on the way to financial security. I cannot emphasize how important it is to have money of your own. Every time you get paid, before you are tempted to spend the money, pay yourself first. If twenty-five percent is too much, put at least ten percent into your savings. Everyone has the ability to save. You can start small and save only $10 per week. Over time, your small deposits will add up.

Women who keep track of their savings often end up saving more. Saving money doesn't have to mean sacrificing fun. Get creative. Save and have fun.

It's not just about saving; it's also about getting pleasure out of spending. You don't need to have a greater amount of money. You just need to spend it differently. Shop smart. Find ways to enjoy what you have even more. Remember building wealth is eighty percent mindset and twenty percent strategy. Once you have the affluent mindset in place, it's easy to implement the strategy of living a balanced life.

PART II

JOURNEYS OF AFFLUENT WOMEN

My goal from Chapter 4 to Chapter 10 is to share motivating and relatable life stories of all kinds of women who attained wealth, so that any woman, anywhere, can read a story and see herself reflected. Although I've changed their names to protect their privacy, these women are shining examples of what we can become if we work hard to shift our limiting mindset. While each woman's story is unique, their messages are universal. They have overcome adversity, gone great distances on their own, lived through different life stages, and developed their own financial roadmap. My hope is that one of these women will inspire you to pursue prosperity.

CHAPTER 4

THE JOURNEY OF
A RISK TAKER

In 1968, my mother Bernice was a successful real estate owner in Hong Kong. One year later, she was a penniless, single parent of four living in a foreign country whose language she did not speak well.

> *"The journey of a thousand miles*
> *begins with one step."*
>
> —LAO TZU

Bernice immigrated to Hong Kong with her parents at age two. She was the only daughter in a family with five sons. Beginning at age five, she had the responsibility of taking care of her younger brothers. Her parents didn't have a lot of money and could only afford to send their sons to school. Her parents favored sons because, in Chinese culture, only sons can pass on the family legacy and inherit the wealth.

Still, Bernice learned to read and count while helping her brothers with their homework.

When Bernice was sixteen, her older brother dragged her to see a handsome young Christian pastor singing and praising God on a street corner. The young pastor caught Bernice's eye, and they quickly fell in love. The couple married when she was just seventeen and had four children. Bernice and her husband worked in a church and made little money. She attended Christian college on weekdays and worked in the church on the weekends. She managed to get her education while raising four children with the help of extended family members. When the church started a school, Bernice received her degree and became the school principal. Over time, the couple saved their money and bought their first house.

The real estate market in Hong Kong began to bloom in the 1960s. On a whim, Bernice and her husband asked her father-in-law if they could borrow a sum of money to invest. They invested in the construction of residential high rises for a small sum of money, and when the units became occupied a year later, the investment doubled and sometimes tripled their return. By 1966, Bernice had a maid and a driver. Her family lived in a brand-new high rise with security guards and doormen. Bernice and her husband had attained wealth. They owned two luxury cars and multiple properties. The church and three schools were also growing. All her children were attending prestigious boarding schools. Life was perfect.

Bernice couldn't have predicted what would happen next. In 1969, in the middle of the night, she received a call from the police, who had her six-year-old son after he climbed a gate at the boarding school and ran away. Bernice couldn't find her husband in the house and immediately summoned her driver to find him. The driver found his car outside of his secretary's apartment, and that night Bernice learned of one of his many affairs. This set off a dramatic chain of events that would change her life forever.

Angry and hurt, Bernice had to stay calm and collect her thoughts. She knew her marriage was over. After careful consideration, Bernice felt strongly that she had no future in Hong Kong as a single mother with four young children. She decided to leave everything behind and take her children, all under the age of twelve, from Hong Kong to Canada. Bernice secretly took the profits of one of their sold properties, valued at 50,000 Canadian dollars, as her nest egg to fund a new life over six thousand miles away.

Unable to speak but a little English and not knowing a single soul, she decided to live in Edmonton, Canada after hearing the province did not have visa requirements for British citizens. Nor did it have sales tax or income tax. Edmonton also appealed to her because of the free education it could offer her children. Upon her arrival, Bernice was very frugal and careful with her money. Without a car, she would take a bus with her children to the grocery store and a taxi home with all the groceries. She rented a two-bedroom apartment in the basement of a four-story building, but only one bedroom was furnished. Bernice would sleep on the couch in the living room and her four children would sleep side-by-side horizontally on a double bed. Being too tall for the mattress, her oldest daughter would have a chair at the end of the bed to rest her legs.

Not long after arriving, Bernice saw an advertisement in a local newspaper for an investment that could provide monthly income. She liked the idea of staying home with her kids while still earning an income, so she contacted the number in the ad. A group of men came to the apartment and convinced her to invest her nest egg in a product similar to a soda vending machine. Unfortunately, these men swindled all her money away, claiming that they lost everything and had to file for bankruptcy. Bernice became a penniless single parent with four children to support.

After losing her nest egg, Bernice was devastated. She spent night and day crying—and needed to figure out what to do next. She was too proud to tell her children, whose ages ranged from four to eleven, what had happened. Yet she had to survive and be a strong leader for them. Thus, she had to pivot.

Bernice found the courage to trust her intuition and inner diva to persevere, so she swallowed her pride and kept this devastating loss to herself. Fortunately, she had put aside enough money to cover living expenses for a year. Desperate for a job that paid well, Bernice enrolled in courses to become a nurse.

There is a Chinese proverb "*neng qu neng shen*" which means one must have the ability to roll with the punches or persevere during difficult times and the ability to level up during good times. She had experienced the good life in Hong Kong but going forward, she had to start all over again. This is the essence of "*neng qu neng shen*."

Bernice's life is an example that wealth and good fortune can be changed in a split second. She worked hard to get her degree and became a school principal in Hong Kong. With smart real estate investments, she became wealthy. She took a risk investing in products that she didn't understand and lost her fortune. So, she went back to school to jumpstart a new career as a nurse, became a homeowner, and helped put her children through college. Bernice retired as a nurse at age sixty-five. Three of her children have advanced degrees, and all of them are financially independent. She has eight grandchildren and continues to be single and financially independent.

CHAPTER 5

JOURNEY OF A LATE BLOOMER

———

Hillary didn't graduate from high school, so how did she become the spokesperson for a publicly traded designer furniture company?

"No one becomes a late bloomer
doing something they hate."

— J.M. OREND

Both of Hillary's parents were immigrants. They met at the Plaza Hotel working in the kitchen. Her father was a cook, and her mother was in charge of the vegetables. They fell in love and got married. Hillary was born and raised in Queens, New York, but she didn't learn to speak English until she went to kindergarten. Both her parents worked in the kitchens of the restaurant, and money was tight. All they ever wanted was for Hillary and her brother to have an education and to be financially secure.

Hillary learned shorthand and how to type before dropping out of high school. She didn't think that a college education was necessary, so she started working. In 1953, Hillary saw an ad in the *New York Times*. "Receptionist wanted for famous architect." She didn't know what an architect was, but it sounded intriguing. So, she went to the employment agency dressed in a hat, gloves, a suit, stockings with the seam straight in the back, all ready to be interviewed. Her only skill was typing 100 words a minute on a manual typewriter. They sent her to the architect's office to interview with his secretary, and she was hired for $55 a week.

A few years later, Hillary replaced the secretary who hired her. Her boss was the editor of a magazine, a writer, and a philosopher more than a designer. He was also an incredible speaker. Hillary would listen very carefully, take notes, or transcribe while he dictated his letters, editorials, and writings. In the beginning, he would have to add punctuation and even spell many of the words. Over time, taking notes and transcribing improved her vocabulary, spelling, and fluency.

She was very young, unsophisticated but photogenic. She became the Girl Friday. Whenever they needed a model, they would ask her to pose. Hillary became the architect's muse for the next twenty-one years.

One of the hardest decisions Hillary had to make was to leave the architect's studio. Things were not the same in the '70s, and she wasn't happy. She had decided to leave, even though she didn't make a lot of money. In fact, Hillary didn't have any retirement savings or health insurance but resigned and took three weeks of vacation. Unfortunately, her employer did not offer health insurance, or any retirement savings plans, so she missed out on savings for retirement for twenty-one years.

Three weeks later, Hillary got a call from a major client of the architect's studio, offering her a job as a salesperson selling high-end furniture in their showroom. She was forty-three years old. She had never done sales before and wasn't sure if she could handle it. But she was willing to accept the challenge. As a salesperson, she would have to sell high-end furniture and help customers find the right purchase for their needs. She had to demonstrate a sound understanding of the latest design trends and the features and benefits of each designer piece of furniture. Years of transcribing the product designs and answering questions on the phone finally paid off. Hillary didn't realize that she had developed a strong knowledge of design concepts, and that she had an extensive network in the architectural and design communities in New York.

She started making sales and taking clients to lunch. "When I told my mama and papa that I was taking a client to lunch at the Plaza, they finally realized how successful I'd become. My father said, 'Oh, can you imagine our daughter. We were in the kitchen, and she is in the restaurant.'"

Hilary is living proof that you don't need a high school diploma or a college degree to become successful. She is a quick learner who developed an artistic eye watching her architect boss. Her role as a secretary was equivalent to the role of an administrative assistant today. After serving as an administrative assistant for twenty-one years, Hilary had to shift her mindset, from being a low salary assistant to a sale commissioned industry expert. Hilary met her monthly sales targets and started saving for retirement in her forties. Her home, which she designed and her husband (a construction worker by trade) built, was featured in *Architectural Design* magazine. When her husband passed, Hillary sold their million-dollar home and moved into a penthouse condo overlooking the water and New York City. Hillary officially retired at age eighty but continues to serve as a consultant, traveling in and out of the country teaching others how to acquire an eye for design—where she tells her story.

No matter where you are in your financial life, like Hillary, it's not too late to start saving for retirement, even in your forties. You might have to save a larger sum of money and in some cases continue to earn income part-time. But it is never too late to start saving.

~~Savings Benchmark ~~

How much do you need to save for retirement?

If you start saving for retirement beginning at age twenty-five to age sixty-seven, aim to save at least fifteen percent of your income before taxes each year. For example, if you make $60,000 annually, contribute $750 per month into a retirement savings account. Using the table in Appendix on page 177, at age forty, you should have $120,000.00 saved [2.0 times your salary of $60,000].

In Hillary's case, she started saving for her retirement at age forty-three with a six-figure commission. Using the table in Appendix on page 179, she will need to save $440,000 [4.4 times her commission of $100,000].

These tables help you determine if you are on track with your retirement savings.

CHAPTER 6

JOURNEY OF AN EARLY BLOOMER

—

Jen is in a private plane sitting next to Jeffrey R. Immelt, Chairman & CEO of General Electric. Will she be the new face or the next CEO in corporate America?

"My mind runs. I can never catch
it even if I got a head start."

—KID CUDI

Jen's parents were immigrants from China and Hong Kong. Her father came to the United States to get his PhD in Mechanical Engineering. He met her mom, who was working in a restaurant. They got married and started to build their life together.

Jen's parents were very frugal and conservative. In the winter, the heat was kept at sixty-two degrees. If Jen was cold, she would wear a winter coat around the house. The lights were always off except in the room they were in. Money was always tight.

Her parents didn't believe in having debt and were very careful and judicious about spending. In fact, her dad was religiously planning to ensure that all three daughters would have enough money to attend college and build a better life. He would struggle between saving for future education and spending so that they did not live beyond their means.

At a young age, Jen knew she could excel academically. She tested into a prestigious magnet school, which completely changed her life. Starting at age fourteen, she would take public transportation from a predominately immigrant neighborhood of Queens, New York for one and a half hours to attend this new school. She would do her homework during the bus ride home. Even though she spent three hours a day traveling, it opened the door for Jen to be on a nationally ranked debate club and to work on new science research at New York University. It really opened her eyes to see different possibilities and new opportunities outside the Chinese American immigrant community.

After graduation, she was accepted into a top nationally ranked university in California, which gave her the freedom to experience life away from home. Her parents paid some of the tuition cost, but Jen had to take out some student loans. They taught Jen to be fiscally responsible and to work hard. Deep down inside, she knew that her impeccable academic excellence from Ivy League institutions would pay off when she became a corporate executive.

Jen believes that one can try to control as much as you can, and fate decides the rest. There's a Chinese proverb, "Things will happen, and you're destined by certain things." Jen accepts whatever will be in her destiny as her fate. But within that box, she can do whatever it takes to shatter the glass ceiling, increase her earning potential, and continue to provide for her family. Jen continues to work tirelessly for even the smallest thing. She prepares and plans for a successful career. In her mind, one's earnings and earning potential is just as important as savings.

Jen was raised in a strict environment that was a training ground for success. She was given responsibility early in life to be independent and be a leader. Her parents emphasized the importance of having an education to improve her quality of life. Hard work was ingrained into her personality. Jen acquired the discipline and grit to persevere at age fourteen.

Today, Jen is a smart, driven, self-motivated, financially savvy corporate executive who climbed up the socio-economic ladder working for publicly traded companies. She is the mother of two children with a supportive husband who is the primary caretaker of their children. Jen is the breadwinner in her family. She wakes up at 5:00 a.m. daily to catch the train to work and does not return home until 8:00 p.m. She works harder than most people. To accommodate her demanding schedule, Jen has a live-in nanny and a part-time housekeeper. At the time of our interview, Jen lives in a luxury home with a swimming pool in an upscale neighborhood and owns two luxury vehicles. Her student loans are paid. She has fully funded her children's college education and is on target for retirement savings.

Jen is a strategic planner. Her mind is constantly racing, seeing new opportunities or possibilities, and preparing for her next career move. She had a detailed roadmap with milestones of when she should finish college, when to get her advanced degree, when to start a career, when to get married, when to have a child, along with a disciplined savings plan for each stage of her life.

~~Mindful Saving Challenge ~~

Disciplined savings is one of the secrets to Jen's success. Before we proceed with the basic concepts of savings, let's explore how you feel about savings.

Does saving money feel good?

Do you like to save money?

Does saving money give you peace of mind? Or help you face the unknown?

Is a penny saved the same as a penny earned?

Are you a good saver?

Does saving money give you independence?

Take some time to journal your thoughts and feelings. Exploring your current attitudes about savings is an important step in improving your net worth.

Ready to unleash your inner financial diva and start saving?

First, do you know what simple interest is?

It is extra money earned on your original investment. For example, Sara deposits $1,000 at a bank at an interest rate of 1.2 percent per year. At the end of the year, she would earn $12 in interest [$1,000 times 0.012].

What is compound interest?

It's' basically "interest on interest"—interest you earn on your initial investment plus all the interest that has accumulated over time, so it makes your investment grow at a faster rate. Suppose Sara deposits $1,000 at a bank at an interest rate of 1.2 percent compounded monthly. At the end of the year, she would earn $12.07 in interest. She earns more money with compound interest.

Have you heard of the Rule of 72?

Rule of 72 is an easy way to calculate how long it will take for your savings or investment to double at a given interest rate if you don't add any more money to your investment. The formula is to take the number 72 and divide it by the interest rate you hope to earn, which gives you the approximate number of years it will take for your investment to double. For example, if you invest $8,000.00 in a mutual fund with an average eight percent rate of return, it will take nine years for your savings to double to $16,000.00. Watch your money double with the Rule of 72.

Why are these concepts important? Rule of 72 serves as a guide for you to measure how well your investment is doing. Simple and compound interest are different ways to earn interest or more money.

Why save? People set aside money so that it can be used later. More often, we save money to reach financial goals such as paying for college education.

Your first savings challenge is to establish an Emergency Fund [if you don't have one yet]. An emergency fund or rainy-day savings is money set aside exclusively to cover the cost of unexpected events such as a job loss or major car troubles. This is your peace-of-mind money when times are good, and you can defend against financial ruin if things turn bad. This fund serves as a personal safety net with a hidden advantage—you get in the habit of putting away money.

How much should you have in the rainy-day fund?

1. Calculate how much you need to feel comfortable. Three months of expenses is a good starting point. For those of you who love numbers, you can figure out how much you should save by adding your mortgage or rent payments, the kids' expenses, food costs, car payments, utility bills, and any other fixed and incidental expenses. Look at your expenses for the past few months and focus on basic needs. Keep in mind that you can cut back on dining out or buying new clothes but don't skip the electric bills.
2. Figure out how much you can save each month. This requires checking your money mind-map. How much is left over after paying all the expenses?

3. Challenge yourself to cut expenses and increase your savings. Are there expenses you can cut back, like the premium channels on your cable television bill or the weekly eating out? Can you work overtime to boost your savings?

Once you decide how much money you can put aside, set up a monthly direct deposit, or create an automatic transfer from your checking account into your savings account. Scheduled deposits will ensure successful savings, and the size of deposits should be determined by what you can afford.

Keep in mind that it takes time and discipline to build an emergency fund. Fight any urge to tap the fund for predictable expenses like car insurance or property tax.

So, go ahead, figure out your expenses and how much money you can put aside each month! Trust me, that information is already on your money mind-map. Just take a quick peek. Your goal is to have six months' worth of expenses saved up, I know it sounds impossible, but I promise you it is doable and life changing. Before long, you will be a disciplined saver like Jen.

CHAPTER 7

JOURNEY OF A FASHIONISTA

———

Emmy is wearing a crisp white shirt, capri pants, and ballet flats, which reminds me of the pedal pushers that Audrey Hepburn wore in the '50s. Even though Emmy has faced her share of financial challenges, somehow, she is different. And that is her greatest advantage.

"Being well dressed hasn't much to do with having good clothes. It's a question of good balance and good common sense."

—OSCAR DE LA RENTA

Emmy was fourteen years old when her family immigrated from Hong Kong to San Francisco, California in 1973. Her father worked as a chef in a Chinese restaurant, and her mother worked in a sewing factory. Their first financial goal was to save money to buy a house. It took three years of hard work and long hours for her parents to purchase their first home for $47,500. But when the family moved in, they didn't have any furniture. After closing escrow, they had $50 left. Money was tight, and they had to make ends meet.

Emmy started working in high school because her parents couldn't afford to buy her the fashionable clothes that she loves. The high school counselor referred many jobs to her such as babysitting and house cleaning. Emmy was paid $15 for cleaning a house but stopped when a man tried to attack her in his home. So, she took on more babysitting jobs.

To save money on tuition, Emmy finished high school one semester early to attend a local community college to fulfill core university requirements. She also lived with her parents while attending community college to save money. After completing two years at a local community college, all the eligible credits were transferred to San José State University. As a third-year university student, she lived in an apartment off-campus, having to pay tuition, rent, and living expenses. Emmy would sacrifice sleep and worked part-time five to six hours a day to make ends meet. At one point, she only took the minimum of twelve units because she was working full-time. It took five years to earn her Bachelor of Arts degree. Emmy had completed the interior design curriculum, but she wanted the housing emphasis, which required completing five additional business classes including business law, affirmative action, and business writing.

Emmy graduated with a 2.75 GPA because of numerous part-time and full-time work. With only a couple hundred dollars in savings after graduation, the next challenge was to start a professional career. Every new position Emmy was interested in required additional relevant working experience, and this led to limited options.

In 1983, Emmy was unemployed with a small college loan (under $5000) and rent to pay. To make ends meet, she would take on odd jobs, from being an administrative assistant in the morning, a counselor for youth in the afternoon, and teaching Chinese on the weekend. She held two part-time jobs and a weekend job. Fortunately, at that time, her parents wanted to rent out the in-law unit in their house, Emmy asked if they would rent it to her. They agreed, and she moved back to her parent's house. Emmy had her own space, her own bedroom, bathroom, and kitchen, but she couldn't afford to pay rent for the first few years. Her parents waived the rent, knowing that she was struggling.

Emmy's first professional job was working part-time at a non-profit agency. Unfortunately, a few weeks later, the non-profit agency lost funding and laid her off. She immediately volunteered to work for another non-profit agency to gain experience, but after a week, she ran out of money to pay for transportation and meals. Being broke taught her a lesson— to never to run out of money. She promised herself that her next paycheck would be set aside for emergencies.

A few months later, a non-profit architecture firm hired her as a housing educator. Emmy immediately paid her parents rent at $400 a month, increasing to $1,000 a month by the '90s. At the time, one thousand dollars was a lot of money. But still, she paid her parents.

The architecture firm offered a retirement plan, and Emmy immediately made the maximum contribution. In her words:

> "When the employer offers you a matching opportunity, it is free money. Why do you want to say no to free money?"

Some employers will match the contributions you make to your retirement plan dollar-for-dollar. If you don't make any contributions, then you would lose the employer match. Emmy started saving for retirement in her twenties. She also paid her student loan two years after university graduation because she wanted to be completely debt-free before saving for retirement.

While Emmy was happy with non-profit work, her love was always fashion. Once she found a stable job, she started investing in her professional wardrobe, even when struggling financially, and was still able to look fashionable and professional.

Her advice is:

> "You don't have to spend a lot of money to look good. I don't buy expensive stuff. I don't like expensive purses. It's my personality."

Emmy bought her own clothes when she was in high school and over time became a smarter shopper. She continues to follow fashion today and has the creative ability to match color. If you gave her ten pieces of basic clothing (not necessarily brand names), she could mix and match them to create a capsule wardrobe. Emmy was known as a fashionista to her peers. She was well dressed and utilized clothes purchased many years previously. She weighed about the same over the years—plus or minus ten to fifteen pounds difference, so all her clothes would still fit. In fact, at our interview, Emmy was wearing a pair of black capri pants that were thirty years old. She had the money to buy a new pair but didn't find anything she liked; instead, she combed through her closet and recreated the desired outfit.

Emmy's personal mantra is:

> "I do not want to spend too much money on expensive clothes and instead invest in good classic clothes with a little bit of fashion. I do not waste money on expensive cars and clothing."

Ms. Fashionista worked her entire life, mostly for non-profit organizations. She was able to retire debt-free at the age of sixty, living off her savings. Her story proves that you don't need to spend a lot of money to be chic.

~~~Mindful Spending Challenge~~

"It is not the man who has too little, but the man who craves more, that is poor."
—SENECA

Are you ready to become a Savvy Shopper like Emmy? Let's work on spending money that aligns with your values and being mindful about living within your means.

Sometimes, shopping isn't always done out of actual need or want. Emotions come into play that can sometimes cloud our judgment. According to a survey from Ebates.com,[3] sixty-four percent of women admit to indulging in this behavior.

Before you buy an item, ask yourself four questions:

1. Why am I buying this?
2. Why am I buying it now?
3. What happens if I do buy it?
4. What happens if I don't?

Then put the item on hold for twenty-four hours (or leave it in your cart for the same amount of time if you're online). If you still want the item after your day has passed, consider it. Chances are, you'll change your mind and realize you don't need it. If you do decide to make the purchase, without

---

3 News, *Businesswire*, April 2, 2013. "Ebates Survey: More Than Half (51.8%) of Americans Engage in Retail Therapy— 63.9% of Women and 39.8% of Men Shop to Improve Their Mood."

thinking twice, a week later write down how you feel about buying it. Even better, if you've purchased a dress, leave the tags on and don't wear it for a week. If you are feeling buyer's remorse, you may be able to return it.

In our culture, we are so used to buying new clothes, gadgets, and knick-knacks instead of repairing what we have or replacing it. Buying less and taking the time to select new purchases seem so strange. To shift your mindset and gain a new perspective, I challenge you to go on a temporary shopping fast on clothes and shoes. Don't buy any new clothes or shoes for thirty days and see how you feel. During the month, keep a little diary to journal your thoughts and feelings. Don't be surprised if you feel the urge to shop on Day 15; just remind yourself to explore the motivation behind your shopping habits and clean your closet instead.

I promise you in thirty days, you will be able to identify your triggers for wanting to go shopping. You will also discover other enjoyable activities to replace shopping.

CHAPTER 8

JOURNEY OF A MAVERICK

———

"Mom, can I get a pair of Levi's jeans?"

Tori can sense her Mom tensing up and watched her with a trace of apprehension.

Her answer was slow in coming. "Why? You don't need it."

"I don't care, I want a pair!" said Tori, her voice rising. "Why can't I get one? You're so cheap!"

Sparks are bound to fly between Tori and her mom on any issues that involve money. Tori spoke her mind and pushed her mom to the edge. If truth be told, Tori will tell you today that her mom was right.

*"I personally believe mavericks are people
who write their own rulebook."*

—ZIAD K. ABDELNOUR

Tori was a teenage mom and high school graduate at the age of sixteen. She grew up in a middle-class background in Bronx, New York. Her mother, Misty, worked as a payroll person for the hospital. It was unusual for a black woman to have an administrative role at the time. Misty managed all the wage garnishments, which gave her a different perspective on saving and handling money.

Her father was a machinist and a hustler; he worked for a power tool company and later became a partner of a tool company. He also owned soda machines in different factories. Every Friday afternoon, Tori and her father would buy sodas, load up the machines, and take the quarters out. At age twelve, it was Tori's job to count the quarters and roll them up into paper coin holders every Friday evening. On Saturday, she would bring the coins to the local merchants in exchange for dollar bills. Tori learned later her father was charging these merchants fees for exchanging the coins for dollar bills, as the banks that could normally provide such a service were closed on Saturdays back then.

Every Monday, her father would leave a stack of money on the kitchen table with a silver spoon on top. Misty would take the money, put a paperclip on the cash, and then put it inside her coat pocket in the closet. The next morning, Misty would deposit the money at the bank. Sometimes Tori would take some money from her mother's coat pocket, knowing that her mother would not miss the cash. Misty ran the household and paid all the bills using her husband's money but saved all the money from her paycheck. She was very meticulous about balancing the budget. When Tori got older, she realized that Misty was the saver and her father was the mindless big spender.

Tori started saving in the third grade. Twice a month, she would deposit all her savings into her account at the bank, but she was not allowed to spend the money. Tori finished high school at age sixteen, but her parents wouldn't let her attend the Massachusetts Institute of Technology, so she started working. As a single mom, she had a great support system. Her Nana, aunt, and father would take her son to activities.

When her son was two, Tori wanted him to attend the Montessori School, which cost about $4,000. Misty wanted him to go to daycare. They decided that Misty would pay for the tuition and Tori would pay for transportation to the school. Tori had to figure out how to attend college and pay for the bus. She got a job as a taxicab dispatcher, working from 11 p.m. to 7 a.m., in order to be home and put her son on the bus.

At age twenty, Tori got a stable government job working for public transit. Her uncle and her father's friends were all working there, so she knew almost everyone who worked at the transit. Now that Tori had money of her own, she started to spend money freely. Even though she was taught to save at a young age, she began to follow the bad habits of her colleagues using credit cards. When the credit card bill arrived, she would write a check but not mail it. The check would be on the dashboard of her car or in her purse. She continued to spend mindlessly using her credit card, thinking that she would have money to pay, but she never paid the bill on time. Over time, her credit became bad, not because she didn't have the money to pay but because the payment was always late. With late payments, interest had to be paid on the amount due, plus the additional late payment fee.

One of her colleagues told Tori about changing her withholding on the W4 to code 99 before going on vacation, so that she would have extra money to spend. So, Tori changed her W4 accordingly, but after her vacation, she didn't remove the code. In those days, one would have gone to the downtown office to make any changes on the W4. The following year, her finances were completely out of control. The Internal Revenue Service was chasing her down for unpaid tax obligations. Now in addition to bad credit, she was at the stage where her wages could be garnished by the Internal Revenue Service. Even though Tori snapped out of the late payment cycle within two or three months, it took over seven years to rebuild her credit. Subconsciously, Tori thought that her mother would be her savior because she knew that her mother had savings and could always bail Tori out. Even though her mother would be in a position to help her out, Tori was too proud to ask.

"I absolutely will NOT ask my mother for a dime!"

As a black woman growing up, Misty was not allowed to have an account in the bank and had to hide the money in a secret place. Sometimes her money could be found under a mattress, in the freezer, or in a jar hidden in the kitchen cabinet. She also did not believe in having a credit card. Tori recalled on one occasion, her mother had saved so much money in cash that when she did try to deposit it in a bank account, she had to meet with the bank manager because she was almost over the FDIC limit, which at the time was $100,000.

Misty passed away at age ninety-three. Her entire life savings was in a passbook bank savings. After paying for all the things for Tori and her grandson for almost sixty years, she still had more than $700,000 in cash. Misty always reminded Tori that people who made the least amount of money are most diligent about savings. Even though Misty never made more than $35,000 per year in her lifetime, she saved more than she ever spent. Financial success is not based on how much money you make but how much you save.

--Debt Free Challenge--

"Never spend your money before you have it."
—THOMAS JEFFERSON

We all know that debt is a reality for almost everybody, but it doesn't define your financial future. Maybe you made bad choices like Tori. Even though she had the money, she neglected to pay her credit card bill and ended up with debt and bad credit. Just imagine being debt-free. Your financial diva is challenging you to live in the present, pay off your debt, and take control of your financial health.

Ask yourself the following questions:

1. How do you feel about your outstanding obligations?
2. Can you only afford to make minimum payments on your credit cards?
3. Do you worry about finding the money to make monthly car payments?
4. Do you borrow money to pay off old debts?
5. Have you used a home equity loan to refinance credit card debts, then run up new revolving balances on your cards?

If you said yes to any of these questions, then it's time to rewrite a new story that tells your adventure of becoming debt-free. Visualize yourself actually living to your full potential with an unlimited amount of success, happiness, and wealth.

Now, let's drill down to focus on the details. Review the Money Mind-map that we created in Chapter 3. Look at how much money you take in and how much you spend. Can you make ends meet on the basics: housing, food, healthcare, and insurance?

There are two types of debt: Secured and Unsecured.

Unsecured debt is not tied to any assets, such as student loans, credit card debt, and medical care bills. If you stop paying your credit card bills or any unsecured debt, the interest and late payment fees continue to accumulate.

Secured debt is tied to an asset, like a car for a car loan or a house for a mortgage. If you stop making payments on your car, the lender can repossess the car. If your car is repossessed, you still have to pay the balance on your loan, plus towing and storage costs. The creditor can sell the car to offset the amount owed. If you stop making payments on your mortgage, the lender can foreclose on your house.

When you are struggling with a significant amount of debt that you cannot repay, you have the option of filing bankruptcy. Bankruptcy is a legal process that involves seeking legal assistance from the U.S. Federal Court to discharge some of your debts so that you get a fresh start financially. Declaring bankruptcy is a serious matter with long-lasting consequences including lowering your credit score, which causes lenders to charge you a higher interest rate. A bankruptcy also stays in your credit history for up to ten years.

For our discussion, we will assume that you are not filing bankruptcy and want to pay back the debt.

Here's how:

Step 1. Take inventory of all your debt to determine how much you owe. List each loan on the worksheet—fill in Name of Credit Card, Total Amount of Debt, APR, Monthly Minimum Payment, Payment Dates, etc. (See Appendix page 181)

Step 2. Determine how much you can pay (take a look at your Money Mind-map—besides must pay items, how much do you have remaining?).

Step 3. If you have trouble making ends meet and you cannot make payments—act now. Contact your creditors immediately. Explain your hardship and work out a modified payment plan that reduces your payments to a more manageable level. Don't worry, I will walk you through what to say.

1. Take a few minutes to copy the Call Log. (Appendix page 180)
2. Did you know that you can negotiate your cell phone, cable, and internet bill? Let's practice negotiating with a bill provider first. Before calling, do some research online about the going rates and competitor prices. Keep in mind that the key to any negotiation is:
   a. Be polite.
   b. Embrace awkward silences when you haggle.
   c. Ask to speak with a supervisor who has the power to override.
   d. If all else fails, threaten to cancel the service.
3. Use the sample script and practice. (See Appendix page 182) When you are ready, pick up the phone. Call your credit card provider and explain your situation. You can:
   a. Request a lower interest rate.
   b. Request to have late fees and over-limit charges waived.
   c. Ask if they can offer a longer repayment period to reduce your monthly payment to an amount that's more manageable. You must know how much you can pay. Do not agree to a loan payment that is higher than what you can afford to pay.
4. Use the sample script as a guide. Be sure to take notes during your conversation, include the date and time of the call and the name of the person you are talking to using your call log. Ask for a letter in writing to confirm the new terms. When the letter arrives, review the document closely to make sure the agreement is correct

before making any payments. Meanwhile, check your credit score each month.

Step 4. Once you have all the APR information (including the new negotiated APR), let's chart a payment path. The general rule of thumb is to put more money on the highest interest loan, so that it gets paid faster. Start with paying the highest interest loan or smallest balance (to boost motivation) but keep paying the minimum on all debts. After one loan is paid off, choose another to pay down aggressively until all bills are eliminated. You'll gain momentum as you put more and more money toward paying down the remaining bill.

In some cases, making a balance transfer from a high-interest credit card into a lower rate credit card may make sense, especially when there's zero-percent financing for the first twelve months. This transfer will give you more time to pay down the loans.

Step 5. You can get help from a debt relief service or credit counseling service.

Debt Settlement Programs—offered by for-profit organizations—will negotiate with your creditors for a settlement amount to resolve your debt—generally a lump sum amount less than the full amount owed. However, creditors have no obligation to negotiate a settlement of the amount you owe. For-profit organizations such as Freedom Debt Relief will charge a fee ranging from fifteen percent to twenty-five percent for their service.

Non-profit debt relief organizations will assist you in developing a Debt Management Plan where you deposit money each month to pay back your debt. The organizations, like American Consumer Credit Counseling, pay your unsecured debts, such as credit card bills, student loans, and medical bills according to a payment schedule. Your creditors may agree to lower your interest rates or waive certain fees. American Consumer Credit Counseling charges a small fee for Debt Management Plans.

Step 6. Debt Consolidation: If you own a home, you can consolidate your credit card bills into one easy monthly payment and lower your cost of credit through a Home Equity Line of Credit loan. But your home will be used as collateral if you default on your payment.

Step 7. Be creative. Use your tax refund or bonus to pay down debt. Look for small ways to save money every day.

Step 8. Break the cycle of recurring debt. Cut up all your credit cards and stop using them. When you're paying off debt, don't add more loans. Do not cancel your cards, just stop using them. It can be tempting to reward yourself by splurging on an expensive dinner or a new smartphone, but just a few purchases can erase all your hard work. Before you buy things, think long and hard before taking on new debt. Keep checking your credit score. You can get your FREE credit score from Credit Karma and create scenarios to see how your improved money habits can change your future credit score.

Step 9. The final step is to set up an automatic payment from your bank account to pay the loan payments now. You can also get a debt repayment calendar from Powerpay online program free. (www.powerpay.org).

Even if you fall into debt because you made poor choices, when you use your Money Mind-map and follow all nine steps, you too can uncover your inner financial diva and become debt-free. Like Tori, ending debt, saving money, and growing your wealth can be your reality.

CHAPTER 9

JOURNEY OF A NEWCOMER

———

Dora is a strong independent woman who does not allow a man to affect her stability or self-confidence. She is not afraid to share her opinions and speak her truth. She creates her own path.

"We travel, some of us forever, to seek other states, other lives, other souls."

—ANAÏS NIN

Dora left Honduras because she was tired of living in a sexist or "machismo" culture of gangs, guns, and violence, where a man's power is often measured in bullets. She came to Massachusetts to visit her brother in 1986, on a visitor's visa as a single mom with a four-week-old baby. Her son was the product of a relationship with a Honduras man that she didn't want to marry. At age thirty-two, she wanted to live independently and raise her son on her own; because in Honduras, men can do anything they want to women including femicide.

Because she and her baby stayed longer than the period allowed by the visa, she was constantly worried about being deported and had to deal with survival. Luckily, she fell in love with her brother's Caucasian business partner and decided to get married to establish her residence status. She was attracted to his demeanor with children; he loved and adopted her son.

Dora was pregnant with her second son before she realized that he was a womanizer. They didn't share the same values in the relationship. When she found out that he was in a relationship with another Latina woman, she confronted him. They tried to restore trust for the next six months, with the help of a marriage counselor. But it didn't help. He cheated on her again with the same woman.

Dora didn't want her boys to be exposed to unfaithful behavior where a man had multiple relationships. She didn't want them to see how disrespectful he was treating her. She confronted him again, ended the relationship, and told him never to come back to their house.

They separated, and Dora filed for divorce. The custody battle was devastating, financially and emotionally. For five years, they went back and forth to court hearings. Dora wanted full legal and physical custody of both children because she was the more stable parent. Dora's main concern was the safety of her boys, and she knew that her soon to be ex-husband couldn't provide a stable environment. The court appointed an attorney to represent the boys. Everyone had to meet with the court-appointed evaluator to determine what custody arrangement would be in the best interest of the children. At that time, Dora was willing to fight until the end for full custody, so she could have mobility in the event she would need to move to another part of the state or out of state.

Her ex-husband was self-employed as a construction worker; thus, he was able to hide his income. Yet, Dora rarely received child support for the two boys. Her ex-husband had the privilege of not showing any income but still had money to spend.

Being the financially stable parent, Dora worked for the state government as a Social Worker. She was the primary breadwinner. She was also the one who was qualified to get a mortgage and the one who carried the health insurance for the family. Yet Dora was new to the culture and financial system. When they brought their first family home together in the late '80s, they had to pay nineteen percent interest for their mortgage because he had poor credit and she didn't have a credit profile. It scared Dora that her husband had a business, but he didn't file taxes when they were married. As a part of the dissolution proceeding, she wanted to make sure that she wouldn't be responsible for his business's financial obligations.

Dora had always been financially responsible. She didn't believe in carrying debt. She paid her taxes. And she had enough foresight during her marriage to put money away without telling her husband as a safety net; just in case something happened.

During the divorce, she worried about being able to keep the house, so that the boys would have a stable home to live. She felt that having a home is an asset that provided stability, built financial equity, and commitment to a neighborhood. Fortunately, she had saved $10,000, which Dora used to pay her ex-husband back for the down-payment to keep the house in her name.

The custody battle went on forever and finally, she gave into sharing custody out of exhaustion.

Dora felt that the court system really failed her as a minority Hispanic woman. Her ex-husband presented himself as a very kind middle-class Caucasian man, while Dora was seen by the judge as a small Hispanic woman trying to bring all kinds of charges against him. She spoke with an accent, and the judge had the preconceived notion that she was uneducated, living on welfare, and needed an interpreter. At the end of the divorce, the judge told her:

"You're lucky that you don't have to pay him alimony."

It infuriates Dora that after paying an outrageous amount of legal fees, her ex-husband didn't even comply with the court order—he didn't show up to take responsibility for the boys every Wednesday after school and every other weekend like he was supposed to.

As a single parent, Dora realized that homeownership is one of the ways to build wealth. When she remarried in 2009, they were able to refinance the house. Ten years later, the same house was worth $120,000 more than what she originally paid.

Dora is planning to retire in a few years. Her sons have graduated from college and are financially independent. She is happily married and continues to be financially independent.

~~Divorce~~

"Divorce is one of the most financially traumatic things you can go through. Money spent on getting mad or getting even is money wasted."
—RICHARD WAGNER

No one gets married with the intention of splitting up, but unfortunately, divorce happens, and it happens often. Going through a divorce can be one of life's most painful experiences. It is an emotionally charged and stressful time for you and your family. You may feel angry, bitter, resentful, and rightfully so. You will experience these feelings intensely, and that is why you need to keep them under control while you make the biggest financial decisions of your life.

As the breadwinner of your family or a stay-at-home mom, are you emotionally and financially ready to end the marriage and embark on a journey to singlehood?

The dissolution of a marriage is all about negotiation. Negotiation requires compromise and making tradeoffs to reach an agreement. Neither you nor your soon-to-be-ex will get everything. Identify the "must-haves" that are important to you and focus on winning them. For example, before you fight over the family home, determine if you can afford to stay in the home. Don't waste time and money fighting for things you don't want out of spite.

Don't be penny-wise and pound-foolish. Choose a trusted team, an attorney, a tax advisor, and a certified divorce financial analyst. Yes, your team of experts is costly. Divorce is not the time to be cheap. Hire the best experts you can afford. Spending a few hundred dollars today in exchange for long-term financial results is worth every penny.

When you have minor children in the marriage, the dissolution of the marriage will take some time—a lot of time. If you and your spouse are fighting over legal and physical custody of the children, the custody battle itself can take up to eighteen years, or until each child turns eighteen. Remember Dora? She was in and out of court for five years fighting over custody of the two boys. In custody battles, plan to pay for long-term legal expenses and other costs.

Don't forget that college funding for your children is shared property. Someone should have stewardship over that fund after the divorce.

The dissolution of a marriage may take months or years to end. The longer the process, the costlier it will be. When you and your soon-to-be-ex decide to end the marriage, be prepared for a contentious and expensive divorce.

If you are contemplating a divorce, start saving for legal fees and collecting all financial documents. (See Appendix on page 175 for the Separation Checklist.) You will need copies of mortgage statements, credit card bills, auto loan statements, joint bank account statements, retirement account statements, life insurance statements, and tax returns. Keep copies of these financial records in a safe place. The more you know about your marital finances, the easier it will be for you to negotiate at the settlement table.

Meanwhile, be proactive. Start opening checking and savings accounts and a credit card in your own name. Also, check your credit score for accuracy. As a single woman, you'll need a good credit score to rent an apartment, buy a new car, or refinance the mortgage to pay the soon-to-be ex. If you are a stay-at-home mom with no credit history or bad credit, you can get a secured credit card to build credit. (See chapter 12 Credit Worthiness on page 108.)

Watch out for joint credit cards opened during the marriage. Credit card companies don't care if you are married or not. Both spouses are responsible for paying back the debt. So even if the court orders your soon-to-be-ex to pay off a joint credit card, but he didn't pay the bill, the credit card company will demand payment from you. Your credit may suffer.

Ending your marriage will substantially change your retirement planning. If you are a stay-at-home mom, you may be entitled to your soon-to-be ex's retirement funds and a portion of his pension. If ten years and one day have passed between saying "I do" and "I don't" to the marriage, you may be eligible for your soon-to-be ex's social security benefits. Moving forward, you will have to figure out how to make your money last for the next ten, twenty, maybe thirty years or more. For some women, it may mean reinventing your skills and working outside the home. So, start planning for your own retirement from a new financial perspective.

During the divorce proceedings, you'll have what seems like a never-ending series of questions, emotions, and decisions to make. But no one expects you to know the answers to all of these. Navigating a successful financial path and a new beginning doesn't have to be traumatic. Remember, Dora didn't have the resources and knowledge that you now have. With a team of trusted advisors on your side, you can create a successful financial roadmap to become a stronger financially healthier woman.

CHAPTER 10

JOURNEY OF A RISING STAR

———

Lori keeps raising the bar for herself and everyone around her. She knows that if she reaches for the stars and gives everything her best shot, she will succeed.

"Remember how far you've come, not just how far you have to go. You are not where you want to be, but neither are you where you used to be."

—RICK WARREN

Lori's mother immigrated to the United States but couldn't bring Lori until her little girl was nine years of age. While Lori's mom worked as a housekeeper, Lori grew up very poor in the Caribbean with no electricity and no indoor plumbing living with her father. But Lori's mom wasn't going to leave her only child behind. After saving for nine years, she sent for Lori to come to live in the United States.

Once arriving, Lori flourished and started attending public elementary school in Brooklyn, New York. Her academics were through the roof and caught the attention of a Connecticut college prep boarding school. Through a scholarship program offered to inner-city kids, Lori had the chance of a lifetime.

The boarding school scholarship only paid for so much. While she used safety pins to squeeze every drop of toothpaste out to make it last longer, her wealthy friends lived the high life, driving BMWs and Mercedes. Though she felt privileged to have an education and was grateful to be able to attend classes with the luxury of having all meals provided, Lori found herself struggling with finances.

Once she earned her high school diploma in 1995, she went on to get a college degree in 1999, where she met her future husband, Roy. They got married in 2002 when she was twenty-three.

After obtaining her law school degree in 2004, Lori thought she was moving farther and farther away from poverty.

She wasn't wrong, but she also wasn't correct.

As college students, they didn't have any savings. Even after Roy started teaching while Lori was still a student in law school, they had accumulated approximately $200,000 to $250,000 in student loans.

Yet Lori felt confident that she was going to get a professional job and a matching income. She was willing to take any job, even as a bartender. No job was below her in order to pay bills and student loans. She didn't want to be lacking, but she had a substantial amount of debt including credit card debt that was used to finance her education.

When Lori got her first professional job, the couple's focus was to get out of debt. It meant sacrifices and tradeoffs. They would not buy a brand-new car, rent an expensive apartment, or spend freely. Everything had to be based on needs versus wants. Up until 2019, they still had not finished paying their student loans but felt very close to freedom. So close that Lori could see her dream of having a really big house. While they could afford a bigger house with their income, and Lori desperately wanted to keep up with the "Joneses," they didn't want to be stretched thin. In keeping to their pact to pay down debt and not feeling the need to impress anyone, they bought a modest house in Connecticut for about $200,000 in 2008.

Instead of the large home, the couple sent their daughter to an expensive high school. They believed the private school education was a worthy investment but still wondered…if they lived in that expensive, large house, would they have been in a better school district? Was the tradeoff of private school offset by living in a larger home?

Like many families, Lori and Roy are constantly struggling to save for their retirement, pay down debt, and pay for private school tuition. They are beginning to accumulate wealth but don't have any affluent role models to guide them. Their greatest challenge is balancing and enjoying their life now while simultaneously preparing for the future.

Lori's drive to get out of poverty is the key to her success. She was willing to take out loans to finance her education because as a college graduate she would have a greater potential lifetime income. Her determination to get a job, even if it wasn't a professional job, showed her grit.

Today, she is a partner in a large prestigious law firm with offices in Connecticut, New York, and Washington, D.C. Lori is listed as a Super Lawyer Rising Star, and received the National Bar Association's "40 Under 40 Nation's Best Advocates" Award. She is on the Lawyers of Color's Hot List and Lawyers of Color—High Achievers, and is also an Adjunct Law Professor—who still lives in a modest house and "got over" keeping up with her colleagues in terms of having a lavish lifestyle.

--Student Loan--

"The best investment you can make is an investment in yourself. The more you learn, the more you'll earn."
—WARREN BUFFET

Getting a college degree is an excellent investment in yourself. It expands your career options, giving you skills and knowledge that will help you in life, no matter what job or career you choose. It also increases your earning potential. Take a look at Lori. She received a Bachelor of Arts in English and worked for two years before enrolling in law school to become a lawyer.

Before going into debt and applying for student loans, figure out how much money you actually need. Here's what you need to know:

1. What Income will you receive while attending school?
   a. Grants
   b. Savings
   c. Scholarships
   d. Job or Work-study
   e. Family Contributions
2. What Expenses will you have while attending school?
   a. Tuition
   b. Room and Board on campus or Rent and Utilities off campus
   c. Books and Supplies
   d. Food and Snacks
   e. Transportation
   f. Phone/Internet
   g. Entertainment
   h. Medical/Dental/Vision Insurance
   i. Personal (Clothing/Laundry/Toiletries)
   j. Other
3. Is there a gap between Income and Expenses? If your income does not cover all your expenses, this is the amount you need to get for a student loan.

Remember that a student loan is a long-term legal commitment that you need to repay with interest. Avoid borrowing more than you need.

After you earn your college degree, hopefully, you will get a higher-paying professional job. Use the grace period or the first six months after graduation to pay other bills before the first payment on your student loan is due. Then set up automatic payments from your bank account monthly to make the student loan payment. If you are unable to make your student loan payment, contact your lender immediately to discuss options to temporarily postpone payments or adjust your repayment plan. Lenders may work with you to pay just the interest, change your payments based on your current income, or allow you to make smaller payments now and bigger payments later. Keep in mind that even if you can temporarily postpone your student loan payment, the interest will continue to accrue and the amount you need to repay will increase.

~~Multiple Student Loans~~

When you have multiple student loans, you may consolidate all your loans into one. Your new lender pays off all your current loans and issues a new loan for the total amount you owe. Your options depend on the type of student loans you have.

1. Federal Student Loan Consolidation: When you have federal student loans, you have the following options:
   a. <u>Free Direct Loan Consolidation Program</u> is offered by the U.S. Department of Education. All your loans are consolidated using a weighted average rate of all the loans (rounded up to 0.125 percent) over the life of your loan. Consolidation makes it easier to manage all

your loans with a single payment, but it doesn't save you money on the interest. However, you can extend the terms of your loan for a lower monthly payment. This process does not require a credit check.

b. Income-driven repayment plans if eligible, sets your monthly payment to ten percent to twenty percent of your discretionary income. Depending on the repayment plan, outstanding loan balances may be forgiven after twenty to twenty-five years.

c. Forgiveness Program: In some cases, the Public Service Loan Forgiveness Program forgives the remaining balance on your student loan after you have made 120 payments (or ten years) under a qualifying repayment plan. (For more info:https://studentloans. gov/myDirectLoan/pslfFlow.action#!/pslf/launch) However, you can be taxed on the forgiven amount. For instance, Hanna graduated from law school with $150,000 worth of student loan debt from multiple creditors. Among many job offers, she accepted a position with Legal Aid At Work in San Francisco (a 501 (c) (3) organization), so that she could consolidate all four of her student loans at four percent, pay the monthly amount of $909.00 for ten years and have a remaining balance of $109,072.92 with interest forgiven.

2. Private Student Loan Refinancing: A private lender repays all your federal and private student loans and issues a new loan based on your creditworthiness. If you have good credit, you can save money and lower your monthly payment by refinancing your student loans at a lower interest rate. Be careful because when you refinance federal loans, they become private loans and will not be eligible for income-driven repayment plans and forgiveness

programs. You have the option to consolidate all your federal student loans and all your private student loans separately.

Keep in mind that repaying student loans takes years and sometimes decades. Take Lori's example; she is still paying off their student loan debt nineteen years later at the time of our interview. So, make sure you set up automatic payments for repayment of your student loan. Pay as much as you can afford. When you get a bonus from work, make an extra payment. Also, when you file your federal tax return, be sure to deduct up to $2,500 a year in interest on federal and private student loans from your income on your federal income tax return. No matter how long it takes to pay back a student loan, it is the best investment you will ever make in your life—who knows, maybe you'll be the next 40 under 40 Superstar in your industry.

CHAPTER 11

BUILDING WEALTH

———

"That some should be rich shows that others may become rich and, hence, is just encouragement to industry and enterprise."

—ABRAHAM LINCOLN

Believe it or not, the financial life of a woman changes every ten years. Each stage of your life will have different money challenges. If there's a roadmap for your financial life, would you follow it?

Looking back, I wish someone had warned me about the different money challenges, the fact that how you live today and the decisions you make will impact your overall ability to enjoy life.

Like a monopoly game, wealth building is a game that can be played to win. Sometimes, money needs to be saved to be a safety net.

My Story

When I was a child, my financial well-being was totally dependent on my parents' financial status. For instance, when I was born, my parents struggled to make ends meet. Whenever I was sick, I had to stay with my mom's cousin because my parents had to work. By the time I was nine, they owned real estate, drove luxury cars, employed live-in nannies and maids. My mom changed our financial picture when we became immigrants in Canada. She lost our family savings and therefore no longer had a safety net. My mom had to learn a new skill and get a job. She became a full-time nurse living from paycheck to paycheck supporting the five of us.

Like most Chinese American immigrant families, my mom believed strongly that a college education would get us out of poverty. Once we had our degrees, we were expected to get a professional job that paid well. Saving for college was a daunting task.

I worked part-time as a teenager with the goal to save for college. I actually worked at Jack-in-the-Box. In those days, when a customer paid, you had to quickly calculate the right amount of change IN YOUR HEAD. This was my first introduction to handling money daily. Hard work paid off and out of high school, I received scholarships, grants, and worked every summer to save money for college. Like Jen, the early bloomer, the responsibility was a good training ground for strong work ethics, discipline, and self-control.

College is a time to be independent, live on your own, and be able to manage your own money. As a college student, I wanted to avoid debt and chose to work part-time four hours a day to make ends meet. I took every job available through work-study and did house-cleaning on the weekends, also. I remember spending only $1 on frozen yogurt or donuts for lunch because I had to pay tuition, rent, utilities, and food. But deep down inside, I knew that the struggle was temporary because someday soon I would get a professional job that paid millions. Some of my friends would sacrifice sleep to work five to six hours a day to graduate within five years. They were willing to take any job, including bartending, to get out of poverty if their plans didn't work out.

Indra Nooyi's Story

Indra Nooyi, former CEO of PepsiCo, talked about coming to America with only $50 in her pocket. She didn't have any money as a college student, not even money to buy clothes. If she saved just $5, she thought that she had gone to heaven. Indra recounted that she worked the graveyard shift as a receptionist to earn the extra fifty cents per hour to pay for food. Being dead poor was a great learning experience. She had learned to be careful with money earned, so that there would be enough money for weekly groceries.

Andrea Jung's Story

There are other options to build wealth, such as starting a business. Andrea Jung, former CEO of Avon, talked about how her grandmother changed her family trajectory out of poverty when she received an informal loan to start a hair salon. My older sister followed a similar strategy by becoming a part-time Avon sales representative to make extra money.

Data from the 2016 Survey of Consumer Finances[4] shows that in families where the head of the household had a college degree, the overall net worth of the family is most likely to be four times more compared to families whose head of household has only a high school diploma.

Remember Jen, the Early Bloomer?

Jen, the Early Bloomer described in an earlier chapter, followed a similar principle, and planned on acquiring prestigious credentials to climb the socio-economic ladder.

What does it all mean?

The truth is that no matter your circumstances or what stage of life you are in, whether you are a student, a single mom, or a business owner, it is never too late to create a financial roadmap to build wealth.

---

4   Board of Governors of the Federal Reserve. "Survey of Consumer Finances." Economic Research. Accessed on April 30, 2020. https://www.federalreserve.gov/econres/scfindex.htm

PART III

CHALLENGES BY THE DECADE

My goal in Chapters 12 to 15 is to provide guidance on how to create your own financial roadmap for financial wellness, while avoiding the hazards ahead so that you are not blindsided.

In each decade, there are financial toolkits to help you manage your financial life. It is not necessary to follow these toolkits in sequential order. You can skip around if the financial topic does not relate to you.

Whether you are beginning your career, early in your career building wealth, in the middle of your career accumulating wealth, or in the pre-retirement stage transitioning into retirement, your financial journey is completely different from every other person. I hope you'll find the tools you need to guide your financial life.

CHAPTER 12

TWENTIES' CHALLENGES

You face a lot of new transitions in your twenties—graduating from college, starting a new career, managing earned money (and debt!), and trying to figure it all out. It can be overwhelming knowing there is so much information out there and being unable to have a strong grasp of what to do or even know where to start.

You may be asking:

"Should I buy a car? Or lease it?"

"How do I know how much of my paycheck I should be using to pay off my loan or credit cards?"

"What are these financial plans my job's asking me to contribute to? Retirement is so far away..."

"Who can I trust to help me plan financially? Can't I just wait 'til I have someone else to do it for me?"

"Isn't investing and planning for older people who actually have the money to do it? I'm just trying to keep up with my bills."

And finally, "There's so much to figure out. I'm going to wait until someone (like parents, spouse, financial experts, etc.) can do it for me. I don't even want to deal with it."

I completely understand; it can be hard to be motivated to find the answers to these questions. The thought of figuring this stuff out on our own (especially if we're not naturally good at math or like the thought of dealing with money) feels like a waste of time. Unfortunately, women who didn't make their finances an "important thing in their life" fail to plan and protect themselves financially. They end up with bigger problems and messes down the road to untangle. Time is lost and opportunities are missed that they can't ever get back. I want to help you avoid that now. In your early twenties, you are barely an adult going through huge changes financially. No worries. I will address each of your questions as we move along together. Trust me, near the end of the decade, you may be set in your career and may have a family.

The most important thing you need to pay attention to is how you earn and save!

You don't have to solve every missing item in your Financial Checklist for your twenties right now. (See Appendix on page 171) You just need to have a plan in place to begin to understand the scope before they become urgent or out of control.

*"In the beginner's mind, there are many
possibilities, but in the expert's, there are few."*

—SHUNRYU SUZUKI

Imagine you're now age twenty; what are your greatest challenges? For the first time, you have a job and your own money. You have so many choices. You want to experience the ability to buy anything you want, at any time, and for whomever, but on credit. While it feels like you have a lot of time before you need to focus on your financial planning, putting it off is actually very harmful to your financial future.

The good news is the *Roadmap to Financial Security* is different for everyone. Some have college degrees and others do not. Some work for companies or corporations and others own their businesses. Some are in debt, and others are debt-free.

Here are some words of wisdom:

If you choose to work for a corporation, our corporate executive who climbed up the socio-economic ladder, Jen, recommends focusing on your earning potential. Develop a career path for salary progression so that you can earn more while enjoying work and career.

Our rising star Lori strongly suggests developing a plan to pay off college debt while balancing the need to start saving.

Tori's strategy was to insist that no matter what you do, make sure you pay your college loan or credit card bill on time. Not doing so would have severe consequences beyond belief.

Regardless of which path you choose, the guiding principle is to maximize your money-flow by spending less than your inflow of money and saving more than your outflow of money. For instance, Jen had a goal to make $500,000 a year to increase her earning potential; while Lori paid an additional $500 per month to her student loan to increase her net worth.

It is imperative that you master the fundamental concept of Mindful Spending.

--Mindful Spending--

Mindful spending is all about using intuition or listening to your inner diva. You know intuitively where money is flowing in your life. Deep down inside, you also know how to be mindful of where your money is going and making simple trade-offs to trim costs every day. Mindful spending gives financial control. You really don't need to have a greater amount of money. You just need to spend it differently and smarter. It's about spending money that aligns with your values.

When you trust your intuition, you'll become mindful about living within your means. You'll naturally become a smart shopper by comparing prices and quality. You'll begin to *consume* less, *subtract* the obvious, and add the meaning of what matters.

Some of you might be thinking BUT... spending habits are difficult to break. Yes, spending habits are difficult to overcome. Keep in mind that if you developed the habit, then you have the power to break it. The first step is to be aware of your spending habits, then combat them by taking small steps.

Track your spending: you can set the maximum amounts you plan to spend each week. Once you reached the allocated maximum, STOP.

Research shows that women feel happier when they make purchases as rewards to themselves. When we're anxious, sad, or frustrated, we go shopping to buy stuff we don't need. Our body has accepted shopping as an effective way to trigger the release of dopamine in our brain's reward system. Even though we feel stressed out, the moment we find something we like, we feel much better. Over time, that association between buying new stuff and the emotional reward gets stronger and stronger, until it's turned into a habit. This can result in cravings to "buy new stuff" whenever we feel particularly bad or good.

If you tend to make impulse buys when you're sad, anxious, or super happy, then:

1. Analyze your individual triggers for wanting to buy stuff.
2. Figure out an activity you could do instead of shopping to have fun and pass the time.

Mindful spending is all about spending your money differently. You don't need to have a greater amount of money. It's about freedom of choice and celebrating small breakthroughs in your spending habits. A penny saved is a penny earned. Everyone has the ability to save. You can start small and save only $10 per week. Over time, your deposits will add up. Even small amounts of savings can help.

Focus solely on the things that matter. The five most important areas of your life are:

1. **Earnings** - Now that you have money coming in, what should you do with it? Check out the Money Mind-map in Chapter 3.
2. **Spending** - You want to have fun and also want to save. How can you juggle bills and cash for what you want *and* need? That's where mindful spending comes in.
3. **Investing** - Starting today will give you a *huge* advantage in the future. Emmy recommends taking advantage of investing through your employer's retirement plan for matching dollars. Or if you're self-employed, start your own retirement plan to save taxes.
4. **Insurance** - If you're renting a house or have an automobile, this is a must. The same for health insurance if you're not already covered by a family plan.
5. **Legal Issues** - You'll want to get familiar with a Will, Power of Attorney, and Healthcare Directive.

Your life is full of transitions starting out, and making a financial plan will help you feel more settled and it'll be easier to manage your savings. I encourage you to take ten minutes today to jot down the ideas and thoughts that you have around your career path and finances. Make it fun, and you'll feel so much better when you finish. Remember, how you live today and the decisions made every day throughout your life will impact your ability to enjoy the life you envision.

> *"The difficulty lies not so much in developing new ideas as in escaping from old ones.*

—JOHN MAYNARD KEYNES

Did you know that women control fifty-one percent of personal wealth in the United States? According to information gathered by Pew Research Center,[5] women represent 45.85 percent of the workforce, and we own thirty percent of private businesses. In fact, women are the primary income source of forty percent of households, just like our rising star Lori and high achiever Jen. The average life expectancy for women is over eighty-one years. A longer lifespan means that our income must last our lifetime, thus we must take control of our finances and plan accordingly. No matter where you are on the roadmap, money matters.

--Financial Assessment --

Are you ready to take a deeper dive into your financial numbers? Let's take a look at your financial situation without blinders. I would love for you to journal and explore answers to the following questions:

---

5   Pew Research Center Social and Demographic Trends website. "Breadwinner Moms." May 29, 2013. Accessed on April 30, 2020. https://www.pewsocialtrends.org/2013/05/29/breadwinner-moms/

1. How important is money in your life?
2. Are you making ends meet?
3. Is your financial life out of control? Maybe deep down inside, you feel you're owed something because of a difficult childhood or some hardship in your life?
4. Do you want to have a good time and not be bothered with serious issues?
5. How do you feel about your role in your current financial situation?
6. Is the debt based on the life that you had?
7. What patterns of behavior have been a part of your habit for handling money?
8. What role did you play in letting this debt accumulate?

Once you have explored what's happening in your financial life, you'll find your triggers.

Everyone acquires some debt along the way. In fact, many low and middle-income students must take out student loans to afford college. Student loans are considered good debt because it increases your earning potential. However, after you leave college, you must repay your student loans with interest, whether you graduate or not.

On the other hand, your financial life is out of control if you're spending more than you're making on a regular basis. Is your checking account frequently overdrawn? Or are you still paying off purchases you made a year ago? Or do you use credit cards to cover everyday living expenses, including groceries?

It's time to start getting out of the past spending habits that can generate debt to move to the present.

Spending consumed in the past can burden the present. This old spending pulls you away from the present because of the unwanted debt. When you owe money you don't have, it adds undue stress and anxiety to life.

To shift into the present:

1. The first step is to admit the part you played in getting to your current financial status. Whether it was habit, circumstance, or something else, understand how you got to where you are now.

   Stop feeling embarrassed about your financial situation. We live in a society that encourages women to spend more. In fact, women are responsible for buying necessities for their children, spouses, and home. We also shop to validate ourselves and to feel better.

2. The second step is to release any negative energy around past spending. Stop being ashamed of your debt and start taking control. Leave the guilt and self-blame behind. Absolve yourself from all the guilt and shame and change your perspective from dwelling on the past to focusing on the present and finding solutions. Forgive yourself.

3. The third step is to stop adding to your debt. You must be willing to make concessions and trade-offs in your life to climb out of the debt that seems to just get deeper and deeper every month. The rule is if you can't afford

it, you can't have it. Avoid buying things you'll end up paying for the rest of your life. It will take some time to crawl out of debt—which requires hard work, perseverance, patience, and motivation. Doing so will help you reclaim the lightness and boundless abundance. When you face the burden that challenges you, you weaken the power it has over you. Our rising star, Lori, had to make payments on her student loans for over eighteen years. She and her husband made sacrifices and trade-offs. They bought the affordable house without stretching. Emmy worked three jobs and paid back her student loans two years after she graduated.

Focusing on living in the present and not being imprisoned by the past will move you forward.

-- Credit Worthiness --

"When prosperity comes, do not use all of it."
—CONFUCIUS

Do you know why credit matters?

In simple terms, credit is the right to buy things now and not pay until later. Having credit often depends on your reputation for paying back your loan. Credit makes it possible for you to borrow money when it is needed.

When you apply for a credit card, cell phone service, or even to rent an apartment, the credit provider needs to know if you're a good risk. Credit card issuers, banks, and merchants use your credit scores to help them decide what terms to offer and the rate to be paid for the loan.

A credit score is a number. A high credit score means you have good credit. A low credit score (below 630) means you have bad credit. A higher score means you're less of a risk and are more likely to pay less for the product or service. An excellent score gives you bargaining power and qualifies you for credit cards with the most attractive rates, rewards points, gifts, and cash-back deals.

300 to 629 Bad
630 to 689 Fair
690-719 Good
720 to 850 Excellent

Good credit saves you money and keeps your interest rates low, so you can afford to buy a house or a car. Remember Dora? She had to pay eighteen percent interest on the mortgage of her house because her ex-husband had poor credit and she was a new immigrant who didn't have any credit profile. Having poor credit hinders the ability to pay bills on time. In Tori's case, she had poor credit not because she didn't have money to pay her bills but was penalized for paying them late.

Here's how it works: Your credit report will show your bill pay history, the number, and type of accounts, how long you had your accounts open, outstanding debt and collection actions. Using a statistical program, creditors compare this information to the loan repayment history of consumers with similar profiles. The scoring system awards points for each factor that predicts who will repay a debt. The total number of points, or the credit score, predicts the likelihood that you'll make payments on time and repay a loan.

The good news is you can always improve your credit score by:

1. Paying your bills on time.
2. Pay more than the minimum balance due. If possible, pay the balance in full.
3. Pay down outstanding balances. Are you maxed out on your credit limits? If the amount you owe is close to your credit limit, your credit score will be affected negatively.
4. Stay away from new debt. Too many new accounts will also negatively affect your score.
5. How long have you had credit? Insufficient credit history affects your score negatively.
6. Keeping outstanding charges at or below thirty percent of your available credit limit will help raise your credit score.

Your credit score is your financial report card. You have the right to get a copy of your credit report from all the national credit reporting companies once every twelve months. Check out:

www.annualcreditreport.com or call 877-322-8228.

*"Money is congealed energy, and releasing
it releases life's possibilities."*

—JOSEPH CAMPBELL

Are you looking to establish credit or build good credit? If so, you need the right financial tools to achieve your goal. The good news is a secured credit card can help. Here's the full scoop on using secured credit cards to build good credit.

What is a secured credit card?

A secured credit card uses money you place in a security deposit account as collateral. A security deposit gives lenders the confidence that you will pay them back, even if you have damaged credit or no credit history. That's because if for some reason you fail to pay your bill, the lender can keep your deposit.

Your credit line is based on your income, your ability to pay, and, in most cases, the amount of your security deposit. For example, if you put $1,000 into the deposit account, your available credit line would be $1,000 but you must have sufficient income and demonstrate your ability to pay. Some credit card companies offer up to $2,500 for the initial deposit, but you can apply to increase your credit line by adding to your security deposit. (However, a secured credit card is not the same as a prepaid card. Your initial deposit is simply collateral and doesn't count toward payments.)

How do secured credit cards work?

A secured credit card works just like a traditional credit card. That means you can use it for everyday purchases as well as for transactions where cash or debit cards may not be accepted—booking a hotel room in advance, for example. Making your monthly payments on time is just as crucial with a secured credit card as with a traditional card. Remember, if you default on your payments, the card issuer keeps your deposit. As long as you pay your balance due in full, you will get your security deposit money back when you cancel your account.

Most secured cards are reviewed periodically. If the review is successful, you may qualify to move to an unsecured credit card and receive a refund of your collateral deposit. When handled properly, you can demonstrate to your credit card issuer and credit reporting agencies that you are a responsible consumer who used credit wisely. Eventually, responsible credit behavior can help you qualify for lower interest rates on mortgages, cars, and other big-ticket items.

Having a secured credit card can help you manage spending and build a stronger financial future.

~~Car Leasing versus Car Buying ~~

"Price is what you pay. Value is what you get."
—ANONYMOUS

You're in the market for a car (either new or preowned vehicle). Not sure if you should buy the car outright or lease it?

Choices that you make will determine how much you end up paying over the life of the car. Aim to buy a reliable car that will last for at least ten years.

1. Down Payment: If you don't have cash to put down, the interest charges on a new car can be substantial. Your down payment determines the amount of your monthly payment.
2. Terms of the Loan: Let's use an example to calculate the monthly payment and determine how much you can afford.
   a. Suppose you are buying a car for $30,000 and need a loan for five years with an annual interest rate of four percent with no down payment. Your monthly payment is $552.50. The total cost of your car is $33,149.72.
   b. Let's assume you have $2,000 cash to put down for a $30,000 car. Using the same terms, a loan for five years at $28,000 with an annual interest rate of four percent. Your monthly payment is $515.66. And the total cost of your loan is $30,939.76. The total cost of your car is $32,939.76 which is $209.96 less than not putting cash down.

3. Buying or Leasing the car: If you want to keep the car for at least ten years, buying a reliable car outright makes sense. Once your car loan is paid in full, the car belongs to you. Keep in mind that when you purchase a car, you are responsible for the maintenance and wear and tear of the car. On a leased car, the dealerships often cover the cost of maintenance. In fact, leasing a car may make sense if you want to keep the monthly payment low and only intend to keep the car for a few years.
   a. Using the same $30,000 car as an example with a $2,000 cash down payment at a three-year loan term.

Your monthly payment to purchase the car is $826.67 per month, for a total cost of $31,760.18.

b. If you lease the car, your monthly payment is $344. In three years, you would have paid $14,384 to use the car. You have the option to return the car or to purchase the car at the residual value. Most cars have a residual value between forty-five percent and sixty percent for a thirty-six-month lease. For a 30,000 car, the residual value can range from $13.500 to $18,000. In other words, adding the amount you already paid in lease payments of $14,384, it can cost up to a total of $32,384 to purchase the car.

Before you decide, do some research. Many car companies offer new college graduates rebates or special financing options. Some employers also offer employee car purchase programs for discounts with car dealerships like General Motors, Volkswagen, and others. They also offer lease options. My advice is to take a look at your Money Mind-map to determine how much you can afford for a monthly payment. Be realistic. Don't forget to add the cost of car insurance to your monthly cost. You don't want to end up struggling to make ends meet.

***Key Takeaways:

At age twenty, your challenge is learning how to balance enjoying your life *now* while paying bills and setting aside money for savings. When you learn to spend mindfully and save consistently, you will avoid credit card debt while building a good credit score. Once you have a good credit score, you can choose to buy or lease a car. Trust your intuition to guide you. You are off to a good start.

CHAPTER 13

THIRTIES' CHALLENGES

There are so many different things competing for your attention (and dollars!) right now—family needs, bills, debt, unexpected expenses, and more. It can feel really overwhelming but you know that now, more than ever, YOU NEED to get a firm handle on what's happening with your finances.

The good news is that there is still time to make it work. With the right Financial Plan, you can become wealthy (and debt-free) a lot sooner than expected!

Money is an important aspect of life that really makes or breaks the type of lifestyle you want (for yourself *and* your family). If you're married or have children, you know how difficult it can be to stay on top of your finances. Navigating all the expenses can leave you feeling like there's just enough to go around... and nothing else.

That is completely **normal.** You're not alone.

Now, if you're doing well financially, kudos to you! You have the advantage of the time to not just manage but grow your wealth.

I get these questions all the time from women trying to figure out their finances.

"How much of my paycheck should be used to pay off my debt?"

"Should I rent an apartment or buy a house?"

"How much should I spend on my wedding?"

"Retirement is so far away... can I really afford to contribute to that right now?"

"If I'm investing, should it be in real estate? Or should I just have a savings account? What's the difference, anyway?"

"Who can I trust to help me manage my finances? Can't I just have my spouse or significant other handle that?"

"We are having a baby; can we afford it?"

And finally, *"I have so many expenses. Which ones do I pay first?"*

I totally understand. We've all been there.

Without a solid financial plan, you end up paying your fixed expenses first, and then at the end of the week, there's nothing left. The thought of trying to learn how to create a "solid financial plan" feels scary, difficult, and—quite honestly—expensive. Where would we find the time or money to do this?

I want to give you some clarity, so you know where to start. The number one thing you need to do is:

Assess where you are in life and know what is ideal for you in this stage. Once you can identify that, you know what's next to look at. (Hint: if you're missing anything ideal, that's where you focus next.)

Remember, you don't have to solve every missing item in your Financial Checklist for the Thirties right now (See Appendix on page 172). You just need to have a plan in place to begin to handle them before they become urgent or delinquent.

~~Homeownership~~

"The habit of saving is itself an education; it fosters every virtue, teaches self-denial, cultivates the sense of order, trains to forethought, and so broadens the mind."
—T.T. MUNGER

Is homeownership something everyone should do?

According to Prosperity Now Scorecard,[6] homeownership is the primary means that 59.6 percent of Asian-American and

---

6   Prosperity Now website. "Scorecard Main Findings" Accessed April 30, 2020. https://scorecard.prosperitynow.org/main-findings

53 percent of black families use to build wealth. Remember Emmy's parents? The first thing they did was buy a home in San Francisco for $47,500 in 1976. In 2019, the same home is worth $1.3 million. The greatest investment for Lori's family was the purchase of their home. Buying a home means investing in an asset that can also help you build roots in the community. Historically, most homeowners who own their property for more than ten years as a long-term investment have seen the value of their investment increase.

Should I rent an apartment or buy a house?

Before buying your first home, consider if renting an apartment or buying a home is best for you financially. Housing is a major expense. In general, the cost of housing should not exceed thirty-two percent of your taxable income. For example, if your income is $60,000 before taxes, you can afford to spend $19,200 year or $1,600 month for rent or a monthly home loan payment. When you rent an apartment, your landlord is responsible for the cost of all the repairs and maintenance of the apartment. Thus, renting is cheaper than buying a home. Renting is not for everyone. To evaluate your unique situation, try the *New York Times* online calculator to see if you should rent or buy. (https://www.nytimes.com/interactive/2014/upshot/buy-rent-calculator.html)

Owning a home is a financial commitment that requires additional funds upfront, such as a down payment for the purchase of the home, closing costs, monthly mortgage payments, home repairs, maintenance requirements, property taxes, and homeowners' insurance. Emmy's parents couldn't afford to buy furniture after spending all their savings on the down payment and closing costs for their home. It was a sacrifice they were willing to make, but look at the list below to consider all the costs when buying a home.

1. The down payment is a portion of the sales price paid to the seller by the homeowner to close the sales transaction. Down payments usually range from three percent to twenty percent of the property value. For example, if Lori and her husband bought their home for $250,000, they would need to pay $7,500 to $50,000 as a down payment. Moreover, you are required to have private mortgage insurance if your down payment is less than twenty percent (or $50,000 in our example).

2. Closing costs are paid by the buyer to purchase the home. These costs include origination fees, discount points, appraisal, credit report, title insurance, attorneys' fees, survey, and prepaid items such as tax and insurance. In general, these costs are between three to five percent of your total mortgage. Using a home of $250,000 with a down payment of $50,000, you will need to borrow $200,000 for the mortgage. The closing costs would be an additional $6,000 to $10,000. You will receive an estimate of these costs from your lender when you apply for a mortgage.

3. The mortgage payment is payable monthly with interest for the life of the home loan. For a thirty-year fixed mortgage loan of $200,000, with a fixed four percent interest rate, the mortgage payment would be approximately $955 per month.

4. Home repairs and maintenance costs will depend on the condition of your home.

5. Property Taxes are due annually to the local government entity. The amount of the tax is based on the market value of your home at a rate determined by the county where it is located.

6. Homeowner's insurance is required to protect you against financial losses in the event of natural disasters or as a result of fire, wind, vandalism, or theft.

The rule of thumb is that housing prices three times higher than your income are affordable. In other words, if your income before taxes is $60,000 per year, a home worth $180,000 is affordable. With the purchase of your first home, you'll continue to build up your good credit rating by paying your mortgage on time to establish a consistent history. Over time, the value of your home will increase, and your wealth will continue to grow.

~~Wedding Plan~~

"It takes as much energy to wish as it does to plan."
—ELEANOR ROOSEVELT

What happens after you say "I do" to the love of your life?

Congratulations! I am so excited for you. I wish you happily ever after.

Your challenge is knowing how to balance your wedding celebration while simultaneously preparing for your future. Let's begin your journey on the right financial path.

Ideally, both of you are willing to create your financial road-map together in the form of a written wedding vow, commonly known as a Prenuptial Agreement.

I can hear what you're thinking: "A Prenup? I don't have enough assets or money to worry about a Prenup."

It can feel that way in the beginning, but your life will change. You may become financially secure and wealthy beyond your dreams (especially if you follow our roadmap to financial success). So, I encourage you to sort through all this stuff in a way that is simple, timely, and even fun!

In simple terms, a prenuptial agreement is a contract entered into by you and your fiancé before marriage. This contract reflects each of your financial assets and liabilities and how each of you will deal with your own premarital assets and liability. To avoid fighting over money, you decide what assets will be held separately and what assets will be held together. You can also define how the two of you will manage your finances together with love and understanding.

Before talking to your fiancé about a prenup, make sure you know the answers to the following:

1. What are your financial goals?
2. What is your attitude about money?
3. What role does money play in your life? Money is very important in marriage. Most couples fight over money two to three times a week.
4. Are you a spender or a saver?

5. How do you want to handle finances? Separately or co-mingled together? If you live in a community property state, everything you acquired before marriage is your separate property. Everything you acquire after marriage is community property that belongs to both spouses. Assume you live in a community property state, if you have substantially more money saved than your fiancé, you may want to keep a separate account. If you open a joint account and co-mingle your savings into this account, you have gifted your money to your fiancé, the money is now community property. No matter where you live, women should always have an account of their own to establish good credit history.

6. Are you comfortable talking about money and finances?

7. What do you want to do with student loans or credit card debt if you or your fiancé have more debt? Our rising star Lori was a law school student when she got married. Her husband was working and knew that Lori had more student debt than he did. Once married, their loan obligations may remain separate or may double if combined. They decided to pay down over $200,000 in debt together.

8. How do you feel about taking on debt as a couple? Lori and her husband didn't want to take on more debt as a couple.

9. What happens if you or your fiancé stops working outside the home?

Your fiancé may not have the same view about money. The goal is to meet at a place of understanding, empathy, and agreement about how differences will be addressed.

When you are ready to negotiate a prenup, find a reasonable meeting place, and set a timeframe for the discussions. Communicate effectively:

1. Think about your concerns.
2. Prepare to listen and understand without interrupting.
3. Be open to new ideas lovingly.
4. Ask for what you want.
5. Look for options that work with each other's best interests at heart.
6. Consider using a trusted advisor as a mediator.

Once you have a collaborative financial road map in place, these financial guidelines will serve both of you as a couple for many years to come.

With your written vows in the form of a prenup in hand, you are ready to work together on the next step.

Creating your Wedding Spending Plan together.

Find out if family members are willing to contribute to funding your wedding. Determine how much the two of you want to spend on the wedding. Maybe you want a Destination Wedding or would rather own a home. Decide first what is non-negotiable: Your first home as an investment in your future together or the wedding celebration or both. Then start a joint savings account to save for the wedding/first home. Consider setting up automatic transfers monthly from your and your fiancé's checking accounts into a separate joint wedding savings account. When it is time for your wedding and/or the purchase of your first home, you will be ready for the expenses and down payment. (Check out the chapter on Home Purchase for more information.)

To plan for the wedding ceremony, use the following industry averages as a guide for a wedding reception:

18 percent on Reception Venue
18 percent on Food
10 percent on Photo/Video
8 percent on Drinks
8 percent on Music
8 percent on Flowers and Decor
7 percent on Attire
5 percent on Emergency Fund [unexpected costs]
3 percent on Wedding Planner [optional]
2 percent on Ceremony
2 percent on Transportation
2 percent on Wedding Rings
2 percent on Beauty
2 percent on Cake
2 percent on Invitations and Paper
2 percent on Favors and Gifts
1 percent on Honeymoon

Feel free to adjust the numbers according to your desires. For example, make trade-offs if both of you would rather spend more on the Honeymoon, then skip the Wedding Planner and spend four percent on your Honeymoon. The average wedding costs about $28,000. The down payment for the purchase of a $250,000 home with three percent down is $7,500. You can have both the wedding and the home but would need to save more. You are starting your lives together.

Make good choices. Do as much or as little as you wish. No matter what you decide, you will live happily ever after when you remain *debt-free*.

~~Baby Preparedness ~~

"The most precious jewels you'll ever have around your neck are the arms of your children."
—ANONYMOUS

Congratulations! You're going to be a mom! Your head is spinning with emotions. You're happy, scared, and worried at the same time.

Are you financially ready for a baby?

Here's a list of things you can do to secure the child's financial future and plan for what is ahead:

1. Health Insurance: expand coverage for the baby and review your policy. Figure out if there are out-of-pocket costs.
2. Baby Registry: Register early so that friends and family can help buy those expensive big-ticket items, such as a baby crib, car seat, strollers, and more.
3. Baby Savings Account: Start saving as early as possible for childcare costs, baby expenses like baby furniture, and day-to-day expenses like diapers and formula. In fact, consider setting up an automatic transfer monthly from your checking account into a separate baby savings

account to grow the savings. When the baby arrives, you will be ready for the extra expenses.

4. New Money Mind-map: Update your Money Mind-map by setting aside a spending category to cover childcare costs. If you plan to be a stay-at-home mom when the baby arrives, start planning for life with one income.

5. College Savings: Add a new savings goal to cover future education costs. If possible, start investing in a 529 college advantage savings plan, where the funds are used for future qualified education expenses. In some states, such as Arizona, Arkansas, Kansas, Minnesota, Missouri, Montana, Pennsylvania, and Connecticut, your contributions to 529 are state tax-deductible. In a 529 plan, your earnings grow federal tax-free and will not be taxed when the money is taken out to pay for college. Your college savings will have the potential to grow the sooner money is invested into the account, also resulting in more savings when it is time for your baby to be in college.

6. Life insurance: Life insurance is designed to protect your family who may depend on you for financial support. In the event that you pass away, life insurance will pay a death benefit or a sum of money to the person you named as beneficiary. The sum of money will help support your dependents. Now is the time to consider purchasing life insurance.

7. Legal documents:
   a. Create a Will: Begin working on the will before the baby arrives. Once the baby is born, you can update the will with the baby's name. You don't need to spend a lot of money or hire a lawyer to establish a will. In

fact, in most states, the Attorney's Bar Associations have free sample wills that you can download and use on their website. When you don't have complicated family assets, you can follow the sample will. (For your convenience see Appendix page 185 for a sample will.)

b. Health Care Directive or Proxy: When you are giving birth, unexpected complications can arise. To prepare for the worst-case scenario, have a Health Care Directive or Proxy on hand. A Health Care Directive or Proxy allows you to appoint someone else to act on your behalf as your agent to make medical decisions. Without it, your medical doctor may be required to give you medical treatment that you would have refused if you were capable of doing so. In most states, the Attorney's Bar Associations have a free sample health care proxy that you can download and use on their website. (For your convenience, AARP provides a free sample health care proxy for each state that you can download. https://www.aarp.org/caregiving/financial-legal/free-printable-advance-directives/.)

c. Social Security: Establish a new social security number for the newborn. In some states, the hospital provides a birth registration form with an option to request a social security card for the newborn. If not, you will have to go to your nearest Social Security Administration's office to apply. If you are concerned that your child's social security number may be subject to identity theft, you can add the social security number to your identity theft monitoring service.

This is an exciting time. I know there is a lot to think about financially, but you are brilliant, and you can sort through all of this in a way that is simple, timely, and even fun.

The best part is it will all be worth it.

***Key Takeaways:

At age thirty, your challenge is juggling bills, unexpected expenses, and getting finances under control. You have time. You don't have to solve everything at once. However, you DO need a plan to ensure that you're taking the small (and big) steps necessary to get everything handled. So, focus on the five most important areas of your life:

1. **Earnings** - Now that you're moving up in your career, what are you doing with your bonuses or raises?
2. **Spending** - The "rent vs. buy" conversation around a home can be a big financial decision you're facing.
3. **Investing** - Are you planning for retirement or other long-term investments? (This is especially important if you have children.)
4. **Insurance** - Proper coverage that protects you is imperative.
5. **Legal Issues** - You'll want to have the right legal paperwork in place to plan for the future.

Assess where you are in your financial life and figure out what is ideal for you. If you are missing anything that you need to plan for, that's where you focus next. Highlight the areas you want to improve on, and jot down any thoughts that come to mind. Remember, you don't have to solve every missing item in your Financial Checklist right now. You just need to have a plan in place to start handling them before they get out of control. Let your intuition guide you.

CHAPTER 14

FORTIES' CHALLENGES

———

At age forty, your challenge is balancing your income across your spending, savings, and investment needs.

While there are still many expenses competing for your money, this is the most ideal time for you to start accumulating wealth. It's the perfect stage to acquire investment property and possibly, if you have children, to help them financially as they get older.

The encouraging news is that you still have a good amount of time before retirement to make it all work. With the right Financial Plan, you can grow your wealth and be prepared for future living expenses.

If you haven't already been saving and investing your money, I know looking at your future can feel scary and worrisome. Upcoming expenses like housing, life events for your children (college, marriage, etc.), medical bills, and other unexpected costs can make you wonder if you have enough set aside to make it through okay.

Retirement is also coming up in the next twenty-two to twenty-seven years. It's a big life transition that needs to be handled sooner rather than later.

You still have time. Even if you weren't financially savvy in your twenties or went through financial hardships in your thirties, you can begin to accumulate wealth to provide a secure future for yourself and your family now.

I often hear women in their forties ask:

"What kind of insurance do I need to keep me covered and safe?"

"How can I protect my assets and grow my wealth?"

"The needs of my family and our household expenses are changing (and growing costlier)! Should I take out another loan or use my savings?"

And finally, *"I'm worried about having enough money when I retire. I don't want to keep working this hard ten years from now."*

At this stage, many of them also struggle with regret. They wish they had started managing their finances in a strategic way earlier. Some of them have made some substantial financial mistakes that set them back farther than they would have liked. More than anything, they all want to be prepared for the future and the financial legacy they want to live and leave.

My recommendation for women in their forties is:

In order to protect and grow your wealth in this stage of life, the first thing you need to do is invest wisely. The second most important thing is to set up your insurance and legal paperwork.

Sometimes they look at me and ask, "What do insurance and legal paperwork have to do with my financial planning?"

Frankly, everything. Protecting yourself, the wealth you build, and the generational wealth you leave behind is so important.

Unfortunately, I know far too many people who put this off until it's too late. People tend to avoid the difficult (and scary) conversation around their mortality, especially since it requires them to involve other people they love in these hard conversations. But it's an inevitable part of life. Even though it may feel far off from where you are now, you need to have a plan around what will happen with your assets. It's worth it to have peace of mind knowing you've set up protection for yourself, your family, and your money.

Inside the Financial Checklist for Forties (See Appendix page 173) I have a full list of Insurance and Legal Issues you'll want to be sure are in place. Don't put it off—you will thank me years down the road.

--Pre-Retirement Checkpoint --

"I have enough money to last for the rest of my life, unless I buy something."

—JACKIE MASON

Congratulations! You made it. It's time to plan how you want to live the rest of your life and determine if you have the financial resources to support the life you envisioned.

Remember, retirement is a journey, not a destination. Planning to live financially secure for twenty to thirty years in retirement can be confusing and overwhelming. No one wants to outlive their income. With the right financial plan, you know what your options are and how to be prepared for what you want in these upcoming years. It's also a time to seriously look at the financial legacy that you want to leave behind.

Have you saved enough for retirement?

If you haven't already been saving and investing your money, looking at your financial future can feel scary and worrisome.

Let's dive deeper into numbers:

A. Do you have a retirement income plan? Where will your money come from? Check what retirement savings and sources of income you can count on. Confirm the following sources for income:

1. Social Security: When you are age sixty-one and nine months old, you can apply for Social Security benefits. You can get estimates of your retirement, disability, and survivors' benefits online by creating an account. Once you have an account, determine your benefit estimate, earnings statement, and Medicare taxes you have paid. Keep in mind that the full retirement age is sixty-seven. If you start taking social security at age sixty-two, you will receive twenty-five percent less than the amount at age sixty-seven. Additionally, your annual cost of living adjustments will be based on a smaller figure (retired income versus working income.) If you wait until age seventy, you will receive thirty-two percent more than age sixty-seven. Thus, the longer you wait, the more money you will get from social security. Every year, changes are made to social security. Be sure to check for new changes annually.

2. Pension: Do you have a pension from an employer? Generally, the employer makes contributions on your behalf. Your worker's pension payments are determined by the length of your working years and the annual income you earned on the job leading up to your retirement. However, your pension payment will be the same every year because there are no cost-of-living adjustments. Take our fashionista Emmy's example. Even though Emmy worked for non-profit organizations her entire career, some of her employers provided a pension, which allowed Emmy to take the income at age sixty.

3. Do you have an Individual Retirement Account (IRA)? When you withdraw money from your IRA, you will pay federal and state taxes, because contributions made were pre-taxed. When Emmy retired at age sixty, she could

withdraw money from her IRA and have federal and state taxes withheld.

4. Do you have a Defined Contribution plan such as a 401k, 403B, or 457? These are retirement savings plans offered by employers. Your contributions made to the plan are tax-deductible and may lower your income tax bracket while your investment grows tax deferred. Some employers will match a certain portion of your contributions. This is the free money that our fashionista Emmy refers to. However, when you withdraw money from any Defined Contribution plans, you will pay federal and state taxes.

5. Do you have a Roth IRA? In a Roth IRA, you pay the income tax upfront, but distributions made after age 59½ from accounts that are at least five years old are tax-free. If you expect to be in a higher tax bracket in retirement, it makes sense to pre-pay the tax using a Roth account.

6. How much savings do you have?

7. Do you have any Guaranteed Income Annuities? These annuities provide a guaranteed income or a fixed payment when you retire. You can choose to receive monthly, quarterly, or annual payments.

8. How much income do your investments generate without touching your principal? Keep in mind that you will pay capital gains taxes when you sell your assets for a profit.

The next step is to figure out how much of your income will be taxed. When you are age 70-1/2, you are required to take the Required Minimum Distribution (minimum amount you must withdraw from your account each year and pay ordinary taxes) from all your retirement accounts and pay the taxes. To make things easier, you can roll all your defined contribution plans to your IRA, so that one Required Minimum Distribution is taken.

B. Retirement Spending plan: The amount of money you need in retirement is based on your spending.

1. Housing expenses: Are you renting or paying a mortgage?
2. Taxes: How much income tax and property tax do you have to pay?
3. Fixed Living Expenses: Collect and review statements or receipts from utilities, phone, cell phone, internet, cable, heating, water, electricity bills, home maintenance, clothing, accessories, groceries, and transportation from the last few months to give you an idea of your average costs. These are must-have expenses.
4. Discretionary Leisure Expenses: You have more time to dedicate to your favorite hobbies, recreational activities, dining out, travel, and anything else you wish. These are expenses that are nice to have.
5. Dream Projects: If you want to pursue lifelong dream projects like starting your own business, writing a book, starting a charitable organization, or just following your passion, make sure you have funding set aside.
6. Healthcare: You are eligible for Medicare at age sixty-five. Medicare covers approximately half of your total health care expenses. You will spend an estimated eleven percent to sixteen percent of your after-tax retirement income on routine health care expenses. You will need supplemental medical insurance for better coverage. Unexpected out-of-pocket medical expenses can deplete your savings. Check out tools like One-Click Health Estimator on the Health Services Review website to

calculate your future retirement health care expenses. (https://www.fairhealthconsumer.org/medical)

7. Long-term care: As you get older, you are more likely to develop chronic and serious medical conditions. According to the U.S. Department of Health and Human Services Administration on Aging statistics last updated October 10, 2017,[7] two out of ten women are projected to have a significant care need for more than five years. In fact, there is a seventy percent chance that the average sixty-five-year-old will require some form of lifelong care. Unfortunately, extended care services are not covered by most health insurance policies. You have the option of purchasing long-term care insurance or life insurance with long-term care coverage to relieve family members from providing caregiving full-time.

Once you figure out your fixed and discretionary expenses, you know how much income you need and where to pull the money from.

C. Balance Sheet Management: Ideally, you are debt-free before you retire or have most of your debt paid off.

1. Outstanding loans: Are all your credit card debt and loans paid off? Continue working until all debts are eliminated.
2. Outstanding mortgages: Figure out when you will make your final mortgage payment so that you will own your home outright.

---

7   A Profile of Older Americans: 2017, April 2018, was developed and distributed by the Administration on Aging (AoA), Administration for Community Living, U.S. Department of Health and Human Services.

3. Outstanding Home Equity Line of Credit: It is a good idea to leave your Home Equity Line of Credit open, only if you have a zero balance. In the event of an emergency, you can use your line of credit.

If you are not financially secure, you might consider pushing back a retirement date a few years and keep working to pay off any existing debt while building up your savings.

D. Insurance Review: Are the insurance policies you have in place sufficient for the rest of your life? If you have dependent children, ask how long your children will need your financial support and plan accordingly. Most women in their sixties without dependents do not need life insurance. Remember our high school drop-out Hillary? She didn't need life insurance because no one depended on her for income. At age sixty-five, you should have income from savings and pensions.

1. Life Insurance–are there better options for seniors? Do you still need life insurance?
2. Medicare strategy and supplement insurance coverage discussed above.
3. How much homeowner's insurance and umbrella policy do you need? When it comes to homeowner's insurance, you need enough insurance to cover the cost of rebuilding your house at the current construction rates. A formula that real estate agents use to estimate the cost of rebuilding is to multiply total square feet of the house by local building cost per square foot. You also need coverage to protect personal belongings inside your home, which includes clothing, furniture, appliances, and electronics.

An umbrella policy refers to the extra liability protection against potential lawsuits that may occur from accidents. It can protect you from damages that you, your family, or pets may cause to other people and cover legal costs of defense, medical bills for others, and damages for liability up to the limits of your policy.

4. Disability Insurance pays benefits when you are unable to work. Most employer plans cover sixty percent of your annual salary. Keep in mind that when you retire but continue to freelance if something happens to you either physically or emotionally to prevent you from working, you will need private disability insurance coverage.

5. Do you have a Health Savings Account (HSA)? A Health Savings Account is a tax-advantaged medical savings account available to participants enrolled in a high-deductible health plan. You make tax-free deposits into the account, which lowers your federal income taxes. The funds in your HSA grow tax-free. You can withdraw the funds at any time to pay out-of-pocket medical expenses (with pre-tax dollars) not paid by your high-deductible health plan. Any money left over at the end of the year rolls over to the next year so that your balance keeps growing.

E. Real Estate Review: Once you retire, do you want to live in the same house? Perhaps you want to live in a warmer climate or closer to family members? Decide where you want to live in retirement.

1. Do you have a strategy for selling your primary residence? If you paid off your mortgage, you will have a lot of equity in your home. You can downsize to a smaller place or

move to a less-expensive neighborhood. The extra money from selling your home and buying a cheaper home can be added to your retirement savings.

2. Do you have a retirement residence strategy? You might consider selling your home and moving into a retirement community where you can get medical and long-term care services.

F. Estate Planning: You worked hard your entire life for everything you own. You have the right to decide what happens to your estate and make your wishes known. Creating a will ensures that your legacy lives on through family and friends. Without a will, the laws of your state of residence (known as intestate succession laws) dictate to whom your property and possessions go. You can organize all your crucial documents, pass on information about all your digital assets along with contact information for your tax advisors, financial planner, and attorney in a letter to your heirs. (See sample Family Love Letter in Appendix page 183.)

Are you emotionally ready to stop working?

When your personal identity is intricately connected to work, you might consider scaling back or working part-time for a few years and ease into a new retirement lifestyle. Use your free time to build up a network of new friends outside of work to do activities with.

Once you've checked off everything we discussed, reached the savings milestone, and feel that you are financially secure, congratulations, you are on target with your retirement goal.

***Key Takeaways:

At age forty, even though retirement may seem far off, now is an opportune time for you to make financial decisions that can set you up for the rest of your life. Think about it. You want to be prepared in advance when it comes to finances. This way, when you *have to* deal with financial issues, you're already set up, so it won't affect your current quality of life. Knowing what's coming up, what you're up against, or what your risks are helps you to plan. And when it's done right, this plan can essentially give you control over your financial future. Keep it simple. Focus on the five most important areas of your life:

1. **Earnings** - These are your peak earning years. Manage your options to grow your finances.
2. **Spending** - If you have children, the cost of their college education (and what it means for you financially) is probably close at hand.
3. **Investing** - Do you have savings and investments that help you stick to your timeline for retirement?
4. **Insurance** - Proper coverage that protects you is imperative.
5. **Legal Issues** - You'll want to have the right paperwork in place to be prepared for the future.

CHAPTER 15

FIFTIES' CHALLENGES

———

At age fifty and onward, you enter a transitional period to assess and calibrate your desired retirement vision. You're faced with planning how you want to live the rest of your life and if you have the correct financial resources to support you doing this. You're still young and have many years ahead.

Bear in mind that retirement is a journey, not a destination. With the right Financial Plan, you know what your options are and how to be prepared for what you want in these upcoming years. It's also a time to seriously look at the Financial Legacy that you want to leave behind.

In your fifties, your work life and career are in a critical stage. Whether you've been at your job for many years or have had several changes along the way, you're transitioning into getting ready to retire. For some of you who love your job so much, now is the time to decide if you ever want to retire.

For most people, because they're not prepared or haven't saved any money, this can feel like a huge panic.

It's not too late. There is hope.

At this stage, you are asking:

"How can I be sure that my future is secure?"

"Is it too late to protect my assets and grow my wealth when my savings are not as big as I'd like them to be?"

"I have some really great plans I'd like to do once I'm retired. How can I make that happen?"

And finally, *"Will I run out of money? I feel like I'm going to have to keep working for the rest of my life."*

Many of people struggle with remorse or despair. They wish they had started managing their finances in a strategic way earlier. Some of them have made financial blunders or had "life happens" with unforeseen circumstances, such as losing their retirement money during the stock market crash, that set them way back.

More often, they all want to be prepared for living in the future and leaving a financial legacy.

The recommendation I give to women in their fifties is:

Design the type of lifestyle you want to live in the next twenty-five to forty years. Look at how much it's going to cost to maintain that lifestyle. Then look at the financial legacy that you want to leave behind when you're gone.

Sometimes they look at me and ask, "How does this help with my financial planning?"

Frankly, everything. Right now, time is of the essence. A great financial plan will include a specific timeline with goals and milestones to help you get there. But like any plan, it's impossible to create this road map if you don't know what you want to accomplish.

Unfortunately, I know far too many people who put this off until it was too late. People tend to avoid the difficult (and scary) conversation around their mortality, especially since it requires involving other people they love in these hard conversations. But it's an inevitable part of life. It's worthwhile to have peace of mind knowing you're set up for a secure future.

NOW is the time to figure out what is attainable with the remaining time, resources, and money you have left. (See Appendix page 174 for checklist.) It's never too late to plan for your financial future.

~~ Aging with Dignity ~~

"Our deepest fear is that we are powerful beyond measure. It is our light, not our darkness, that frightens us."
—MARIANNE WILLIAMSON

Aging with dignity and grace is all about planning for challenges that come with serious illness, disability, and aging. It doesn't matter if you have a modest bank account or a small house or a lucrative business and a long list of assets, planning for the inevitable can be overwhelming and difficult. Yet planning for the inevitable is an unavoidable part of life. It is vital to put your affairs in order, especially as you age, so you can be in control over what happens when that time comes.

Here's a list of things to consider:

1. Do you prefer to live at home? There are many services, options, and helpful solutions available to help you stay active, happy, and independent as you age at home. Technology such as medical alert systems, medical tracking gadgets, medical dispensing gadgets, and home alarm systems promote security and enhance your daily life. You can hire in-home services to provide cooking, cleaning, housework, and running errands.
2. If you decide to live at home, you might need to make your home more age-appropriate friendly, such as adding a grab bar or a removable shower-head in the bathroom, a wheelchair-accessible ramp, an adjustable bed, scooters, stairlift, and a wider entryway. You can rent or purchase products to make daily chores and activities easier when your mobility is impaired.
3. Do you want residential care to live independently at home? If your health becomes an issue, you can hire a licensed home health nurse to provide the medical monitoring and therapy to main your health or recovery.
4. Do you want to transition to an assisted-living facility? Assisted living facilities provide room and board and some assistance with activities of daily living. They have medical professionals on staff.

5. Do you want to transition to a senior living facility? A senior living facility is a retirement community or senior housing community for most people age fifty-five and older. These living arrangements may not offer home care services but offer social connections and activities for seniors who do not want the responsibilities of living alone.
6. Do you want to sell your home? You may consider downsizing your home rather than deal with the challenges of home maintenance or move closer to family members.
7. What is your Medicare strategy? Medicare is the federal health insurance program available at age sixty-five and older.
8. Do you want to continue driving? Driving gives you independence, freedom of mobility, and convenience, but there comes a time when you need to reduce or stop driving altogether. Public transportation, taxi, and Uber are cost-efficient alternatives. In some cities, you may be eligible for paratransit.
9. Do you prefer selling or gifting your vehicle?
10. Do you want to create a family wealth mission statement? A family wealth mission statement defines your values and your purpose for wealth. For example: "We want our financial decisions to allow family members to find their passion and pursue it with excellence."
11. Who will take care of your pets?
12. In the event you become incapacitated, who will be your guardian? Think of a responsible, caring, and loving person who will take care of you physically.
13. In the event you become incapacitated, who will manage all financial assets, including paying your bills? Think of a financially savvy person.

The most important thing is to have a health care proxy in place so that someone like a trusted family member can make decisions on your behalf. That trusted family member will be your care coordinator who works with your caregiver and manages your resources, money, and taxes. Let him or her know in advance your care plan and a discharge plan in the event of a surgery.

Your golden years can be the best years of your life. How you choose to live will determine how much money you will spend. Maintaining a healthy and active lifestyle will determine how much money you will need for healthcare costs. Focus on the things you can do and enjoy. Age gracefully. Experience this chapter of your life to its fullest.

--Expect the Unexpected--

"The trick is not to die waiting for prosperity to come."
—LEE IACOCCA

Losing a loved one is devastating. You feel numb. You feel the pain, loneliness, and panic. You are under very severe pressure.

But you are not alone. Everyone suffers the loss of a loved one—a father, mother, sibling, spouse, or friend. But no one is ever prepared for it, even if you see it coming for a long time. Nothing can prepare you for the loss of a loved one— absolutely nothing. You are not ready when it happens.

Give yourself permission to grieve. Feeling your grief is not a sign of weakness. Just the opposite. Trying to be "strong" prevents healing. What you are feeling is normal and necessary. Those feelings will stay with you until you let them out. When you accept and feel your loss, you will begin the healing process. Work through your pain. Feel it. Accept it. Talk about it. The pain will go away, but it will return again and again.

Part of your mind is telling you to do things you normally do even though your life has turned upside down. You realize that many of the decisions that you made together now rest on you alone. While you may want to bury your head in the sand, subconsciously you know that important financial decisions must be made. Decisions that will affect your financial future as a single woman.

When you are under extreme stress, avoid making life-changing decisions. Give yourself time. You will know when it's time to get on with your life. Talk to your trusted advisors and focus on the immediate financial tasks. Consider all your options and continue with your day-to-day routine as much as possible before making any major changes.

You will have questions and concerns about:

1. A Will: If you are the executor of your spouse's will, you must probate the will in court. In the event that your spouse dies without leaving a will, then the property must be shared according to the state rules of intestacy.
2. Life Insurance: If your spouse was employed, check with the human resources department of his employer to see if

he had any life insurance. Contact your insurance agent if you purchased private life insurance. You will need an original death certificate to claim benefits.

3. Survivor Benefits: You may be eligible for Social Security spousal benefits and Veteran's Administration benefits for military veterans and employer benefits depending on your age and your spouse's employment history. If you are over age sixty at the time of his passing, you may be entitled to survivor benefits in addition to a one-time death benefit from Social Security.

4. Retitle Assets: Change the title to your home, bank accounts, brokerage accounts, and car to your name only. Also, contact the Department of Motor Vehicles to cancel your spouse's driver's license.

5. Bills and Loans: Check your online banking profile, checkbook, files of bills, and loan statements. Some may be in your name, your spouse's name, and some held jointly. Contact providers to remove your spouse's name.

6. Cancel Subscriptions: Terminate gym memberships, club memberships, professional magazine subscriptions, and professional association memberships that you won't use.

7. Healthcare: If you were covered under your spouse's policy, you will need your own policy either through your employer if you are working or a private plan. If you are over age sixty-five, you may be eligible for premium-free Part A of Medicare if you or your spouse worked and paid Medicare taxes for at least ten years. Even if you are a stay-at-home mom with no work history, you may qualify for Medicare benefits based on your spouse's work record. Contact Medicare at 1-800-MEDICARE for more information. https://www.medicare.gov/

8. Credit Reports: Send a letter to all three credit reporting services, TransUnion, Equifax, and Experian, to request adding a notation on spouse's file indicating: "Deceased—do not issue credit." Also, request that a credit report of your spouse be mailed to you. In the letter, provide your name, address, and relationship to the deceased, his date of death, his date and place of birth, his social security number, his residence for the past five years, your marriage license, and his death certificate.

9. Retirement: Review the investments in your portfolio to determine if it will meet your financial goal. Start planning for the rest of your life. For example, decide if you want to move or continue to live in the home you shared with your spouse. It may mean that you need to find meaningful work or relocate to a different area.

10. Estate Planning: It's time to update your will and estate plan along with identifying new beneficiaries to replace your spouse. Update the beneficiaries to your retirement plans and life insurance policies.

That's all you have to do to settle your financial obligations.

No doubt, your life will continue to shape itself around the feeling of pain and loss. The loss will always be there. Get comfortable with ambiguity. Don't stress out over things that are not under your control. You will gain clarity as you move forward. From this day forward, you are responsible for your own life. The rest of your life is already happening. Plan for it according to your needs and wants. Manage your finances to support the lifestyle you deserve. I promise you that you will become stronger through your loss.

***Key Takeaways:

At age fifty, you are worried about outliving your assets. The best part is that you can still do something about this, *without* feeling hopeless or panicked. Here are the five most important areas of your life and money decisions:

1. **Earnings** - These are your peak earning years. Maximize your contributions to your retirement plan.
2. **Spending** - How can you more closely watch your spending so you can save and invest more money?
3. **Investing** - Set up a financial timeline to make sure you're getting the most out of all your investments.
4. **Insurance** - Proper coverage that protects you is imperative.
5. **Legal Issues** - You'll want to have the right paperwork in place to be sure all your wishes around health, wealth, and quality of life are honored.

Time is of the essence. You are in charge of your own destiny. Plan your financial future now.

CHAPTER 16

EPILOGUE

---

*"You can't connect the dots looking forward;
you can only connect them looking backward.
So, you have to trust that the dots will
somehow connect in your future."*

—STEVE JOBS

My financial life has certainly seen its fair share of peaks and valleys. There are times when I was struggling to make ends meet and times when I had more money in the bank than I ever imagined. But my defeats are outshadowed by my successes.

It has taken me many difficult years to build my life into what it is today. I have a career in law and finance, a degree in Economics, and a Juris Doctorate in law. I am a Certified Financial Planner, a Certified Divorce Financial Analyst, and a Certified Retirement Plan Specialist. I am divorced and happily remarried with four children. Life is good, and the dots finally make sense.

I started working when I was sixteen because I knew I had to earn my way through college. I worked at Jack-in-the-Box as a cashier. When a customer paid, I had to quickly calculate the exact amount of change in my head. So, I started handing money on a daily basis. Hard work paid off, and out of high school, I received scholarships, grants, and worked every summer to save money for college.

In my second year of college, I rented an in-law apartment unit in Berkeley Hills. I was so excited to be living in my own space that I painted the place eggshell white with a hint of peach. My landlord sued me in small claims court that I breached the rental agreement. The judge ruled in my favor and told me that I was entitled to punitive damages, but I did not seek punitive damages. At that moment, I decided that I would apply to law school and learn everything I ever needed to know.

When I was accepted into law school, my mom said to me, "Why waste your time? You'll never finish law school. Why don't you just get married?" I felt devastated that she wanted me to rely on a husband to secure my livelihood instead of supporting my decision to further my education.

I was young and naïve at age twenty-three. After my first year in law school, I decided to marry an older man I thought was my best friend and mentor. I thought my mom would be happy that I followed her advice, but when I told my mom I was getting married, she replied, "I told you you'll never finish law school." She also disowned me for marrying someone who is Caucasian. I felt wounded by her harsh criticism and actions. It seemed that no matter what I did, my mom was never supportive.

I have always been a rebel. I just didn't know it. On the outside, I am calm and dignified. I kept a lot to myself, bottling it all up.

I didn't know at the time that I had married a malicious childcare teacher. I knew that he had a bad temper, which would turn violent, but he also had a bad childhood. I told myself that things would get better. I made excuses. I didn't want to be a failure at marriage. I thought I could fix it. Each time he physically hurt me, I would justify it. And so, like many other women, I became a silent victim of domestic violence. I didn't tell anyone, not my best friend, not my sisters, no one. I was ashamed, embarrassed, and felt powerless. I could just hear my mother saying, "I told you not to marry him. "

Like most perpetrators of domestic violence, he would apologize after each incident and bring offerings. After I graduated from law school, I got pregnant. When my son was born, I didn't trust anyone to take care of him. Especially if childcare workers were like my abusive husband, so I chose to be a stay-at-home mom. I would take projects working transcribing depositions. The violence got worse when I became a mother of two young children with a successful home-based business of transcribing depositions.

I started working as an in-house corporate counsel when my children were old enough to tell me about their experiences in daycare. I remember my little daughter would tell her friends that her mommy was a liar while trying to pronounce "lawyer."

Then one day, my husband made the mistake of throwing my baby girl like a cowbell to physically crush me. At that moment, I found the courage and rage to fight for my life. I did not want my children to watch their mom get beaten up. The rebel in me fought back, and I walked out with only $20 in my pocket.

The ongoing custody battle and division of assets proved to be a devastating financial hit. I decided to represent myself to stop incurring more attorney fees. I gave him all my possessions, assets, and investments to save my own soul and walked away with our debt. Deep down in my heart, I knew I would have financial security and financial independence one day because I was now FREE. I broke free from an abusive relationship and now had the freedom to live my life on my terms. I am the author of my own life story and the architect of my destiny.

During the dissolution process, I lost my job as a corporate counsel because the insurance industry was downsizing. So, I started working as a temp, making appearances in court for other attorneys, taking up projects, and making ends meet while juggling childcare. Each unique job I took provided me with new experiences that improved my résumé and taught me different areas of law along the way.

Life is full of surprises.

After years of being a single mother, I met my soulmate while working at a pharmaceutical company. We got married, I got pregnant again, and we moved to the east coast. I still didn't trust anyone with my babies and chose to be a stay-at-home mom again with two young children only thirteen months apart.

Being a mom is the most difficult job in the world. It is much easier to work at a job outside the home. My youngest did not sleep through the night until he was three years old. After being sleep deprived for three years, I decided my children needed to socialize with others at daycare. I wanted to join the workforce without taking the grueling Bar Exam again. When I saw the job description for a financial advisor, I knew I could pass the Series 7 exam based on my personal finance experience.

The lessons I learned didn't come easy. But some things you just can't be told. They must be experienced.

Had I not been a silent victim of domestic violence watching my first husband use my daughter as a weapon to hurt me, I would not have had the courage to break free and take control over my destiny.

Had I not struggled with money as a student in college and law school, I would not appreciate the value of a dollar.

Had I not learned to manage, build, and protect my money, I would not be able to leave my abusive marriage. Building wealth is eighty percent mindset and twenty percent strategy.

Had I not studied economics in college, I would not have the confidence to start a career in finance.

Had I not had these experiences and challenges in my life…
I would not be writing this book.

> *"Success is the child of audacity."*

—BENJAMIN DISRAELI

Well, what do you think? Having read the life stories of Gigi
(the tool shop owner), Bernice (the risk-taker), Hillary (the
late bloomer), Jen (the early bloomer), Emmy (the fashionista), Tori (the maverick), Dora (the newcomer), and Lori
(the rising star), what do you think? Could changing your
money mindset and developing a financial roadmap radically
change your financial life? What would happen if you chose
to be bold and take financial responsibility?

Neither you nor I can answer that question until you try it.
I know that countless affluent women who choose to take
control of their destiny have reached financial success.

Consider Lynn's example, Lynn married her husband and
immigrated to the United States. Her prince charming husband treated her as a princess and took care of all financial
matters for her until he was unable to, due to an unfortu-
nate accident. In her sixties, Lynn had to completely take
over financial control for the first time, and she did it. It's
never too late to learn. You can manage your own money
and step into your power. It doesn't matter where you are in
your journey of life. You can change course, hit restart any
time, and take control of your destiny in pursuit of financial
independence.

I wrote this book for you. I hope it changes your financial life. And if it does, please give this book to someone else, your sisters, your girlfriends, your coworkers, your family, or your loved ones. I truly believe that when each of us answers the call to be affluent women, doing what we are passionate about, we will make a fortune. Who knows? Together we may see a better financial future for women from all walks of life.

REFERENCES

Prologue

Salam, Maya. "Money Is Not Just for Men," In Her Words, *New York Times*, June 14, 2019. https://www.nytimes.com/2019/06/14/business/sallie-krawcheck-gender-gaps.html.

Chapter 3

Yates, Stephanie R., "Research Brief: Financial Socialization" AFCPE *Standard Newsletter*, 4th Quarter 2019. https://www.afcpe.org/news-and-publications/the-standard/2019-4/research-brief-financial-socialization/.

Chapter 7

Ebates Survey: More Than Half (51.8%) of Americans Engage in Retail Therapy—63.9% of Women and 39.8% of Men Shop to Improve Their Mood." News, *Businesswire*, April 2, 2013. https://www.businesswire.com/news/home/20130402005600/en/Ebates-Survey-51.8-Americans-Engage-Retail-Therapy%E2%80%94.

Chapter 11

"Survey of Consumer Finances." Board of Governors of the Federal Reserve. Economic Research. Accessed April 30, 2020. https://www.federalreserve.gov/econres/scfindex.htm.

Chapter 12

"Breadwinner Moms." Pew Research Center Social and Demographic Trends website. May 29, 2013. Accessed April 30, 2020. https://www.pewsocialtrends.org/2013/05/29/breadwinner-moms/.

Chapter 13

"Scorecard Main Findings." Prosperity Now website. Accessed April 30, 2020. https://scorecard.prosperitynow.org/main-findings.

Chapter 14

A Profile of Older Americans: 2017, April 2018, was developed and distributed by the Administration on Aging (AoA), Administration for Community Living, U.S. Department of Health and Human Services.

ACKNOWLEDGMENTS

———

In your own way, each of you has been instrumental in helping me bring this book to life. I am forever grateful to:

Evelyn Fong	Nan Santiago
Winnie Wong	Marianne Markt
Marilyn Fardella	Joriz Tiberi
Daniel Lam	Denise Kelly
Katie Flashner	Ava Villegas
Sarah Paikai	Denisha Ferguson
Shelly Vides	

Last but not least, I thank my husband and children for putting up with me and for giving me the time and space to write this book.

AUTHOR'S NOTE

When I started this publishing journey, I never knew how difficult it would be to put pen to paper. After two years, I finally began writing but I had no idea that sharing my story meant reliving the trauma that was buried deep inside me. Thus, it has been cathartic. But writing this book also meant being honest and vulnerable to stand in the truth of who I am.

I want to thank Gigi (the tool shop owner), Bernice (the risk-taker), Hillary (the late bloomer), Jen (the early bloomer), Emmy (the fashionista), Tori (the maverick), Dora (the newcomer), and Lori (the rising star) for challenging me to own my voice.

My hope is that our collective stories help change your financial future.

If this book has helped you in any way, please consider writing a review. Reviews are one of the most powerful things you can do to help this book reach other women in need of guidance to take control and own their wealth. Let's invite others to join this exclusive club of affluent women.

Thank you so much. ~ Kiena Lee

APPENDICES

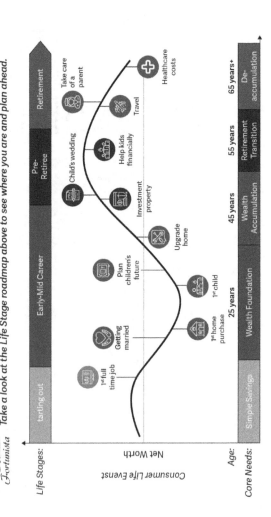

Your Life Events and Financial Decisions

Your finacial needs will change at different stages of your life.
How you live today and the decisions you make everyday throughout your life will impact your ability to enjoy the life you envision.
Take a look at the Life Stage roadmap above to see where you are and plan ahead.

Fortunista

Life Stages:

| tarting out | Early-Mid Career | Pre-Retiree | Retirement |

Net Worth

Consumer Life Evenst

- 1st full time job
- Getting married
- 1st home purchase
- 1st child
- Plan children's future
- Upgrade home
- Investment property
- Child's wedding
- Help kids financially
- Travel
- Take care of a parent
- Healthcare costs

Age: 25 years · 45 years · 55 years · 65 years+

Core Needs:

| Simple Savings | Wealth Foundation | Wealth Accumulation | Retirement Transition | De-accumulation |

CHECKLIST – TWENTIES

Fortunista

At age 20, the challenge is to balance enjoying your life today while simultaneously prepare for your future. It's never too early to start planning.

Use the following Checklist to help identify important financial considerations:

1) Earnings:
- ☐ Develop a career plan for salary progression so that you can earn more while enjoying your work.
- ☐ Start saving and investing 10% or more every paycheck.
- ☐ Take advantage of investing through employer's retirement plan for matching dollars. If you are self-employed, set up a retirement plan.
- ☐ Develop a plan to pay-off college loans while balancing the need to start saving.
- ☐ Envision a target retirement date.

2) Spending:
- ☐ Evaluate the need versus the temptation to buy the new car, rent the expensive apartment and spend freely.
- ☐ Pay yourself first by saving 10% or more every paycheck.
- ☐ Avoid the expense of debt when using a credit card.

3) Investing:
- ☐ Save for an Emergency Fund with at least six months of living expenses.

- ☐ Once Emergency Fund is established, contribute as much as you can afford into a retirement plan.
- ☐ With each salary increase, increase your contributions to a retirement plan.
- ☐ Once your student loans or debt are paid off, increase your contributions to retirement.

4) Insuring:
- ☐ Do you have health and auto insurance?
- ☐ Do you need Renter's Insurance?

5) Legal Issues:
- ☐ Do you have a Will so that your wishes will be honored?
- ☐ Do you have a Power of Attorney so that your financial affairs will be managed if you become disabled?
- ☐ Do you have a Healthcare Directive to designate who will be authorized to make medical decisions for you if you are incapacitated, what types of treatment you would want and whether you wish to receive life-sustaining medical treatment?

Your Life Events and Financial Decisions

Fortunista

Your finacial needs will change at different stages of your life.
How you live today and the decisions you make everyday throughout your life will impact your ability to enjoy the life you envision.
Take a look at the Life Stage roadmap above to see where you are and plan ahead.

Life Stages: tarting out | Early-Mid Career | Pre-Retiree | Retirement

Net Worth

Consumer Life Event:
- 1st full time job
- Getting married
- 1st home purchase
- 1st child
- Plan children's future
- Upgrade home
- Investment property
- Child's wedding
- Help kids financially
- Travel
- Take care of a parent
- Healthcare costs

Age: 25 years | 45 years | 55 years | 65 years+

Core Needs: Simple Savings | Wealth Foundation | Wealth Accumulation | Retirement Transition | De-accumulation

CHECKLIST - THIRTIES

Fortunista

At age 30, the challenge is to balance enjoying your life today while simultaneously prepare for your future.

Use the following Checklist to help identify important financial considerations:

1) Earnings:
- [ ] Manage your career to advance, earn more and enjoy your work.
- [ ] Add the money from raises and bonuses to investments.
- [ ] Make the maximum contributions to employer retirement plans and invest additional earnings in Roth IRA and non-deductible IRA.
- [ ] Protect current and future earnings through health insurance, long-term disability insurance and life insurance.
- [ ] Access your retirement target and evaluate contributions to retirement plans and long-term investments.

2) Spending:
- [ ] Maintain your savings and investing disciple of paying yourself first before paying expenses.
- [ ] Consider purchasing a home as an investment

3) Investing:
- [ ] If you have children, consider adding savings into a College Savings Plan.
- [ ] Balance income to spending, savings and investing especially when family expenses will compete for your investible dollars.
- [ ] Retirement is 25 to 35 years away. Evaluate your investment strategy to make sure it aligns with your financial goals and objectives.

- [ ] Maximize your contributions into retirement plan, especially if you are self-employed.

4) Insuring:
- [ ] Do you have health, auto and life insurance?
- [ ] Do you need Long-term Care Insurance?
- [ ] Is your Liability insurance sufficient to protect your assets from lawsuits?
- [ ] Do you need Umbrella liability offered through your Property & casualty insurers for liability coverage on fire, theft auto, boat etc.

5) Legal Issues:
- [ ] Do you have a Will so that your wishes will be honored?
- [ ] Do you have a Trust?
- [ ] Do you have a Power of Attorney so that your financial affairs will be managed if you become disabled?
- [ ] Do you have a Healthcare Directive to designate who will be authorized to make medical decisions for you if you are incapacitated, what types of treatment you would want and whether you wish to receive life-sustaining medical treatment?

CHECKLIST - FORTIES

Your Life Events and Financial Decisions

Your finacial needs will change at different stages of your life.
How you live today and the decisions you make everyday throughout your life will impact your ability to enjoy the life you envision.
Take a look at the Life Stage roadmap above to see where you are and plan ahead.

Fortunista

Life Stages: tarting out | Early-Mid Career | Pre-Retiree | Retirement

Net Worth

Consumer Life Events:
1st full time job · Getting married · Plan children's future · 1st home purchase · 1st child · Upgrade home · Investment property · Child's wedding · Help kids financially · Travel · Take care of a parent · Healthcare costs

Age: 25 years | 45 years | 55 years | 65 years+

Core Needs: Simple Savings | Wealth Foundation | Wealth Accumulation | Retirement Transition | De-accumulation

CHECKLIST - FORTIES

Fortunista

At age 40, you start accumulating wealth: time to acquire investment property and possibly pay for child's wedding or help your children financially.

Use the following Checklist to help identify important financial considerations:

1) Earnings:
- [ ] This is your peak earning years. Maintain Savings and Investing discipline, manage bonuses and stock options.
- [ ] Consider Long-term Disability Insurance to protect your earnings in the event of a disability.
- [ ] Access your retirement target

2) Spending:
- [ ] Paying for College education expenses? Avoid sacrificing your future retirement by using retirement contributions toward education. Keep in mind that Individual Retirement Accounts [IRA} and 401k are not included in student federal financial aid calculations.
- [ ] You can get student loans for tuition, but there's no loans for retirement.

3) Investing:
- [ ] Develop a comprehensive investment plan factoring in all savings and investments, with targeted timeline to retirement and your risk tolerance.
- [ ] Balance income to spending, savings and investing especially when family expenses will compete for your investible dollars.
- [ ] Evaluate your investment strategy to make sure it aligns with your financial goals and objectives.

- [ ] Retirement is 15 to 25 years away, determine if your investment performance is in alignment.

4) Insuring:
- [ ] Do you have life insurance?
- [ ] Do you need Long-term Care Insurance?
- [ ] Is your Liability insurance sufficient to protect your assets from lawsuits?
- [ ] Do you need Umbrella liability offered through your Property & casualty insurers for liability coverage on fire, theft auto, boat etc.

5) Legal Issues:
- [ ] Do you have a Will so that your wishes will be honored?
- [ ] Do you have a Trust?
- [ ] Do you have a Power of Attorney so that your financial affairs will be managed if you become disabled?
- [ ] Do you have a Healthcare Directive to designate who will be authorized to make medical decisions for you if you are incapacitated, what types of treatment you would want and whether you wish to receive life-sustaining medical treatment?

CHECKLIST - FIFTIES

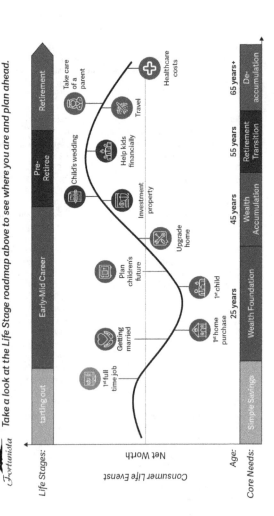

Your Life Events and Financial Decisions

Your financial needs will change at different stages of your life.
How you live today and the decisions you make everyday throughout your life will impact your ability to enjoy the life you envision.

Take a look at the Life Stage roadmap above to see where you are and plan ahead.

Fortunista

Life Stages: Starting out | Early-Mid Career | Pre-Retiree | Retirement

Net Worth

Consumer Life Event

- 1st full time job
- Getting married
- 1st home purchase
- 1st child
- Plan children's future
- Upgrade home
- Investment property
- Child's wedding
- Help kids financially
- Take care of a parent
- Travel
- Healthcare costs

Age: 25 years | 45 years | 55 years | 65 years+

Core Needs: Simple Savings | Wealth Foundation | Wealth Accumulation | Retirement Transition | De-accumulation

CHECKLIST - FIFTIES

Fortunista

Beginning at age 50 onward, you are in a transitional period to assess and calibrate your desired retirement vision.

Use the following Checklist to help identify important financial considerations:

1) Earnings:
- [ ] This is your peak earning years. Maintain Savings and Investing discipline, manage bonuses and stock options with your retirement target in mind.
- [ ] Consider Long-term Disability Insurance to protect your earnings in the event of a disability. The chance of experiencing a disability increases with age.
- [ ] Maximize your contributions: Individuals age 50 onwards can contribute an additional $1000 to IRA, Roth IRA, $3000 to SIMPLE IRA, $6000 to 401k and 403B plans.

2) Spending:
- [ ] If possible, redirect former tuition payments to retirement investments.
- [ ] Watch your spending closely to determine where you can save money and invest more money.

3) Investing:
- [ ] Now is the time for an investing sprint. Maximize your contributions to various investment vehicles. At age 50, contribute an additional $6000 per year to many employer retirement plan and an additional $1000 to IRA.
- [ ] Develop a comprehensive investment plan factoring in all savings and investments, with targeted timeline to retirement and your risk tolerance.

- [ ] If you retire at age 55 or older, you can take penalty-free distributions from your employer's defined contribution plan, but still pay taxes on the distributions.
- [ ] At age 59.5, you can take penalty free distributions from IRAs and employer retirement plan, but still pay taxes on the distributions.
- [ ] Consider consolidating various retirement and investment accounts.

4) Insuring:
- [ ] Do you have life insurance?
- [ ] Do you need Long-term Care Insurance? The older you are, the more expensive the premium.
- [ ] Is your Liability insurance sufficient to protect your assets from lawsuits?

5) Legal Issues:
- [ ] Do you have a Will so that your wishes will be honored? Is it updated?
- [ ] Do you have a Trust? Is it updates?
- [ ] Do you have a Power of Attorney so that your financial affairs will be managed if you become disabled?
- [ ] Do you have a Healthcare Directive to designate who will be authorized to make medical decisions for you if you are incapacitated, what types of treatment you would want and whether you wish to receive life-sustaining medical treatment?

SEPARATION CHECKLIST

Fortunista

Immediate Precautionary Action:

- Cancel joint credit cards and charge accounts
- If you co-signed or guaranteed a loan for your spouse, contact the lender to disclaim liability for any future loans.
- Appraise assets [optional]
- Terminate any assets held under Joint Tenancies (if you want to avoid allowing your spouse to receive the property in its entirety in the event of your death).
- Obtain "freeze" orders on assets and on the removal of your child(ren) from the state {unless state law provides for such orders automatically when a divorce action is filed)
- If warranted, obtain a Protective Order against abuse
- Do not put the child in the middle of your dispute or undermine your spouse' relationship between the child and the other parent (assuming that other parent is not abusing the child)

Documents Needed:

- Bank Statements: Checking, savings, CDs, money market accounts
- Birth Certificates of minor children · Brokerage account statements
- Checkbooks

- Business co-ownership agreements
- Credit card statements
- Disability related documents
- Marriage license
- Prenuptial agreement
- Real Estate deeds and tax records
- Vehicle registration and insurance records
- Health Insurance policies, statement or bills
- Immigration and citizenship documents
- Life insurance policies and premium payment records
- Military service records
- Pension records
- Retirement account statements
- Social security records
- W-2 from showing wages for current year
- Workers' compensation paperwork
- rust Agreements
- Buy-Sell Agreement
- Wills and Power of Attorney
- Healthcare Directives or Proxy
- Long term care policies
- Prior year Income Tax Return
- Loan statements

FIN FITNESS ROADMAP

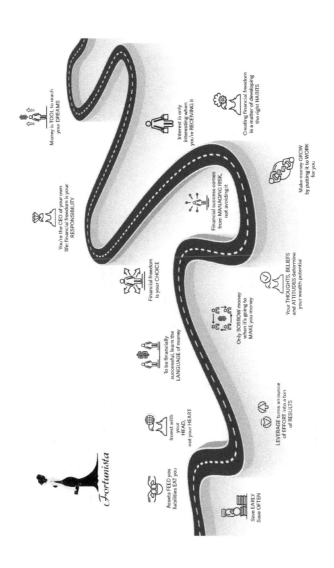

Fortunista

Assets FEED you
liabilities EAT you

Invest with
your
HEAD,
not your HEART

Save EARLY
Save OFTEN

To be financially
successful, learn the
LANGUAGE of money

LEVERAGE turns an ounce
of EFFORT into a ton
of RESULTS

Only BORROW money
when it's going to
MAKE you money

Your THOUGHTS, BELIEFS
and ATTITUDES determine
your wealth potential

Financial Freedom
is your CHOICE

Financial success comes
from MANAGING RISK,
not avoiding it

Make money GROW
by putting it to WORK
for you

You're the CEO of your own
life: financial freedom is your
RESPONSIBILITY

Money is TOOL to reach
your DREAMS

Interest is only
interesting when
you're RECEIVING it

Creating financial freedom
is a matter of developing
the right HABITS

JPM SAVINGS BENCHMARK

Saving

Retirement savings checkpoints

Current age	$30,000	$40,000	$50,000	$60,000	$70,000	$80,000	$90,000
	Checkpoint (x current household income)						
25	0.4	0.4	0.5	0.6	0.8	0.9	1.1
30	0.7	0.8	0.9	1.0	1.2	1.4	1.5
35	1.1	1.2	1.3	1.5	1.7	2.0	2.1
40	1.6	1.8	1.9	2.0	2.4	2.6	2.9
45	2.2	2.4	2.5	2.7	3.1	3.5	3.7
50	3.0	3.2	3.3	3.6	4.1	4.5	4.8
55	3.9	4.1	4.3	4.6	5.2	5.7	6.1
60	4.9	5.2	5.5	5.8	6.6	7.2	7.6
65	6.4	6.8	7.0	7.5	8.4	9.1	9.7

How to use:
- This analysis assumes you would like to maintain an equivalent lifestyle in retirement.
- Household income is assumed to be gross income (before taxes and savings).
- Go to the intersection of your current age and your closest current household income.
- Multiply your salary by the checkpoint shown. This is the amount you should have saved today, assuming you continue contributions of 5% going forward.
- Example: For a 40-year-old with a household income of $50,000: $50,000 x 1.9 = $95,000

MODEL ASSUMPTIONS

Annual gross savings rate: 5%*

Pre-retirement investment return: 6.0%

Post-retirement investment return: 5.0%

Inflation rate: 2.0%

Retirement age —
- Primary earner: 65
- Spouse: 62

Years in retirement: 30

*5% is approximately the U.S. average annual savings rate

This chart is for illustrative purposes only and must not be relied upon to make investment decisions. J.P. Morgan's model is based on J.P. Morgan Asset Management's (JPMAM) proprietary Long-Term Capital Market Assumptions (10-15 years) and an 80% confidence level. Household income replacement rates are derived from an inflation-adjusted analysis of Consumer Expenditure Survey (BLS) data (2013-2016); Social Security benefits using modified scaled earnings in 2019 for a single wage earner at age 65 and a spousal benefit at age 62 reduced by Medicare Part B premiums. For more details, see slide 15.

Consult with a financial advisor for a more personalized assessment. Allocations, assumptions and expected returns are not meant to represent JPMAM performance. Given the complex risk/reward tradeoffs involved, we advise clients to rely on judgment as well as quantitative optimization approaches in setting strategic allocations. References to future returns for either asset allocation strategies or asset classes are not promises or even estimates of actual returns a client portfolio may achieve.

J.P.Morgan
Asset Management

JPM SAVINGS BENCHMARK

Retirement savings checkpoints

Current age	$100,000	$125,000	$150,000	$175,000	$200,000	$250,000	$300,000
	Checkpoint (x current household income)						
25	0.2	0.3	0.5	0.7	0.8	1.0	1.2
30	0.7	0.9	1.2	1.4	1.5	1.8	2.0
35	1.4	1.6	1.9	2.2	2.4	2.7	2.9
40	2.2	2.5	2.9	3.2	3.4	3.8	4.1
45	3.2	3.6	4.0	4.4	4.7	5.2	5.4
50	4.4	4.8	5.4	5.9	6.2	6.8	7.1
55	5.9	6.4	7.1	7.7	8.1	8.7	9.2
60	7.7	8.3	9.1	9.8	10.3	11.1	11.7
65	10.1	10.8	11.8	12.7	13.3	14.3	14.9

How to use:
- This analysis assumes you would like to maintain an equivalent lifestyle in retirement.
- Household income is assumed to be gross income (before taxes and savings).
- Go to the intersection of your current age and your closest current household income.
- Multiply your salary by the checkpoint shown. This is the amount you should have saved today, assuming you continue contributions of 10% going forward.
- Example: For a 40-year-old with a household income of $100,000: $100,000 x 2.2 = $220,000.

MODEL ASSUMPTIONS

Annual gross savings rate: 10%*

Pre-retirement investment return: 6.0%

Post-retirement investment return: 5.0%

Inflation rate: 2.0%

Retirement age –
- Primary earner: 65
- Spouse: 62

Years in retirement: 30

*10% is approximately twice the U.S. average annual savings rate

This chart is for illustrative purposes only and must not be relied upon to make investment decisions. J.P. Morgan's model is based on J.P. Morgan Asset Management's (JPMAM) proprietary Long-Term Capital Market Assumptions (10-15 years) and an 80% confidence level. Household income replacement rates are derived from an inflation-adjusted analysis of: Consumer Expenditure Survey (BLS) data (2013-2016); Social Security benefits using modified scaled earnings in 2019 for a single wage earner at age 65 and a spousal benefit at age 62 reduced by Medicare Part B premiums. For more details, see slide 15.

Consult with a financial advisor for a more personalized assessment. Allocations, assumptions and expected returns are not meant to represent JPMAM performance. Given the complex risk/reward tradeoffs involved, we advise clients to rely on judgment as well as quantitative optimization approaches in setting strategic allocations. References to future returns for either asset allocation strategies or asset classes are not promises or even estimates of actual returns a client portfolio may achieve.

J.P.Morgan
Asset Management

JPM SAVINGS BENCHMARK

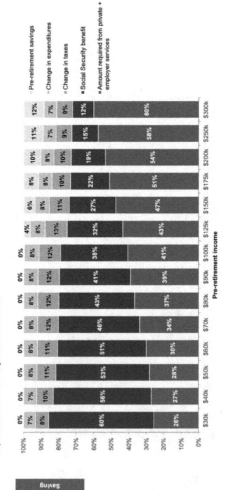

Income replacement needs vary by household income | 15

Replacement rate detail by household income

Legend:
- Pre-retirement savings
- Change in expenditures
- Change in taxes
- Social Security benefit
- Amount required from private + employer services

	$30k	$40k	$50k	$60k	$70k	$80k	$90k	$100k	$125k	$150k	$175k	$200k	$250k	$300k
Pre-retirement savings	0%	0%	0%	0%	0%	0%	0%	0%	4%	6%	8%	10%	11%	12%
Change in expenditures	7%	7%	8%	8%	8%	8%	8%	8%	8%	8%	8%	8%	7%	7%
Change in taxes	8%	10%	11%	11%	12%	12%	12%	12%	13%	11%	10%	10%	9%	9%
Social Security benefit	60%	56%	53%	51%	46%	43%	41%	38%	32%	27%	22%	19%	15%	12%
Amount required from private + employer services	26%	27%	28%	30%	34%	37%	39%	41%	43%	47%	51%	54%	58%	60%

Pre-retirement income

Saving

Source: J.P. Morgan Asset Management analysis, 2019. Household income replacement rates are derived from an inflation-adjusted analysis of: Consumer Expenditure Survey (BLS) data (2013-2016); Social Security benefits using modified scaled earnings in 2019 for a single wage earner at age 65 and spousal benefit at age 62 reduced by Medicare Part B premiums. The income replacement needs may be lower for households in which both spouses are working and the second spouse is an individual; benefits are greater than their spousal benefit. Single household income replacement needs may vary as spending is typically less than a two-spouse household; however, the loss of the Social Security spousal benefit may offset the spending reduction. Percentages and values may not sum due to rounding.

J.P.Morgan
Asset Management

15

JPM SAVINGS BENCHMARK

Annual savings needed if starting today

Saving

Start saving age	$30,000	$40,000	$50,000	$60,000	$70,000	$80,000	$90,000
			Savings rate (x current household income)				
25	7%	7%	8%	8%	9%	10%	10%
30	9%	9%	10%	10%	12%	13%	13%
35	12%	12%	13%	13%	15%	16%	18%
40	15%	16%	17%	18%	20%	22%	24%
45	22%	23%	24%	25%	28%	31%	33%
50	32%	34%	35%	38%	42%	46%	49%

MODEL ASSUMPTIONS

Pre-retirement
investment return: **6.0%**

Post-retirement
investment return: **5.0%**

Inflation rate: **2.0%**

Retirement age:
- Primary earner: **65**
- Spouse: **62**

Years in retirement: **30**

How to use:

- Go to the intersection of your current age and your closest current household income.
- This is the percentage of your current household income you should contribute annually going forward if you have $0 saved for retirement today.
- Example: A 40-year-old with household income of $50,000 and $0 saved for retirement today may need to save 17% every year until retirement.

Important things you need to know:

- Modest forward-looking returns may require higher savings going forward.
- Values assume you would like to maintain an equivalent lifestyle in retirement.
- Household income is assumed to be gross income (before taxes and savings).

This chart is for illustrative purposes only and must not be relied upon to make investment decisions. J.P. Morgan's model is based on J.P. Morgan Asset Management's (JPMAM) proprietary Long-Term Capital Market Assumptions (10-15 years) and an 80% confidence level. Household income replacement ratios are derived from an inflation-adjusted analysis of Consumer Expenditure Survey (BLS) data (2013-2016). Social Security benefits using modified scaled earnings in 2019 for a single wage earner at age 65 and a spousal benefit at age 62 reduced by Medicare Part B premiums. For more details, see slide 16.

Consult with a financial advisor for a more personalized assessment. Allocations, assumptions and expected returns are not meant to represent JPMAM performance. Given the complex risk/reward tradeoffs involved, we advise clients to rely on judgment as well as quantitative optimization approaches in setting strategic allocations. References to future returns for either asset allocation strategies or asset classes are not promises or even estimates of actual returns a client portfolio may achieve.

J.P.Morgan
Asset Management

JPM SAVINGS BENCHMARK

Annual savings needed if starting today

Start saving age	$100,000	$125,000	$150,000	$175,000	$200,000	$250,000	$300,000
	Savings rate (x current household income)						
25	11%	12%	13%	14%	14%	15%	16%
30	14%	15%	16%	18%	18%	20%	21%
35	18%	20%	21%	23%	24%	26%	27%
40	24%	26%	29%	31%	32%	35%	36%
45	34%	37%	40%	43%	45%	48%	51%
50	51%	54%	59%	64%	67%	72%	75%

MODEL ASSUMPTIONS

Pre-retirement investment return: **6.0%**

Post-retirement investment return: **5.0%**

Inflation rate: **2.0%**

Retirement age:
- Primary earner: **65**
- Spouse: **62**

Years in retirement: **30**

How to use:

- Go to the intersection of your current age and your closest current household income.
- This is the percentage of your current household income you should contribute annually going forward if you have $0 saved for retirement today.
- Example: A 40-year-old with household income of $100,000 and $0 saved for retirement today may need to save 24% every year until retirement.

Important things you need to know:

- Modest forward-looking returns may require higher savings going forward.
- Values assume you would like to maintain an equivalent lifestyle in retirement.
- Household income is assumed to be gross income (before taxes and savings).

J.P.Morgan
Asset Management

Saving

17

JPM SAVINGS BENCHMARK

Unless otherwise indicated, all illustrations are shown in U.S. dollars.

Past performance is no guarantee of comparable future results.

Diversification does not guarantee investment returns and does not eliminate the risk of loss.

Indexes are unmanaged and an individual cannot invest directly in an index. Index returns do not include fees or expenses.

The **S&P 500 Index** is widely regarded as the best single gauge of the U.S. equities market. This world-renowned index includes a representative sample of 500 leading companies in leading industries of the U.S. economy. Although the S&P 500 Index focuses on the large cap segment of the market, with approximately 75% coverage of U.S. equities, it is also an ideal proxy for the total market. An investor cannot invest directly in an index.

The **Barclays Capital U.S. Aggregate Index** represents securities that are SEC-registered, taxable and dollar denominated. The index covers the U.S. investment-grade fixed rate bond market, with index components for government and corporate securities, mortgage pass-through securities and asset-backed securities. These major sectors are subdivided into more specific indexes that are calculated and reported on a regular basis.

Bonds are subject to interest rate risks. Bond prices generally fall when interest rates rise.

The price of **equity securities** may rise or fall because of changes in the broad market or changes in a company's financial condition, sometimes rapidly or unpredictably. These price movements may result from factors affecting individual companies, sectors or industries, or the securities market as a whole, such as changes in economic or political conditions. Equity securities are subject to "stock market risk," meaning that stock prices in general may decline over short or extended periods of time.

Investing in **alternative assets** involves higher risks than traditional investments and is suitable only for sophisticated investors. Alternative investments involve greater risks than traditional investments and should not be deemed a complete investment program. They are not tax efficient and an investor should consult with his/her tax advisor prior to investing. Alternative investments have higher fees than traditional investments and they may also be highly leveraged and engage in speculative investment techniques, which can magnify the potential for investment loss or gain. The value of the investment may fall as well as rise and investors may get back less than they invested.

Opinions and estimates offered constitute our judgment and are subject to change without notice, as are statements of financial market trends, which are based on current market conditions. We believe the information provided here is reliable, but do not warrant its accuracy or completeness. References to future returns are not promises or even estimates of actual returns a client portfolio may achieve.

This document is a general communication being provided for informational purposes only. It is educational in nature and not designed to be a recommendation for any specific investment product, strategy, plan feature or other purposes. By receiving this communication you agree with the intended purpose described above. Any examples used in this material are generic, hypothetical and for illustration purposes only. None of J.P. Morgan Asset Management, its affiliates or representatives is suggesting that the recipient or any other person take a specific course of action or any action at all. Communications such as this are not impartial and are provided in connection with the advertising and marketing of products and services. Prior to making any investment or financial decisions, you should seek individualized advice from your personal financial, legal, tax and other professional advisors that take into account all of the particular facts and circumstances of your own situation.

JPMorgan Distribution Services, Inc. member FINRA.

J.P. Morgan Asset Management is the marketing name for the asset management businesses of JPMorgan Chase & Co. and its affiliates worldwide.

J.P.Morgan
Asset Management

Fortunista

CALL LOG

Date of Call	Time	Name of Rep	Discussion

Fortunista

REPAYMENT
WORKSHEET

Name of Credit Card	Total Amount of Debt	APR	Minimum Monthly Payment

Fortunista

SAMPLE NEGOTIATION SCRIPT

———

Hi, I'm committed to paying off my credit card debt next week and I would like to get a lower APR. In order for me to pay off my debt quickly, I need a lower APR. Other credit card companies are giving me rates at half of what you're offering. Can you lower my rate by at least forty or fifty percent?

I've been a customer for over ___ years, and I would prefer not to switch credit card companies. I am getting offers from other credit cards giving me 0 percent introductory rates for twelve months and half the APR that you're offering. Is it possible for you to match other credit cards' rates? Or can you go lower?

Fortunista

LOVE LETTER TO
MY FAMILY

—

Dear Loved Ones:

In an attempt to simplify matters for you, I have written this letter to provide you with the necessary information when the time arises:

Having trusted advisors is a critical part of my planning. You will need to contact the following people:

Accountant: Name, address, phone, email

Attorney: Name, address, phone, email

Employer: Name, address, phone, email

Financial Advisor: Name, address, phone, email

Life Insurance Agent: Name, address, phone, email

Health Insurance Agent: Name, address, phone, email

Casualty and Auto Insurance Agent: Name, address, phone, email

Mortgage Holder: Name, address, phone, email

Pension Benefit:

Here's my list of Assets: Statements of Investments, Bank Statements, Credit Card Statements, Savings Statements, and a list of all personal property owned.

I have signed this Family Love Letter on _(date)_____

This letter is not intended to replace or supersede my will or any other estate planning documents.

_____

Signature

Fortunista

SAMPLE WILL

LAST WILL AND TESTAMENT

of

_____

(Full Legal Names)

_____

(Identification / Social Security Number/s)

_____

_____

(Address)

1. Declaration

I hereby declare that this is my last will and testament and that I hereby revoke, cancel and annul all wills and codicils previously made by me either jointly or severally. I declare that I am of legal age to make this will and of sound mind and that this last will and testament expresses my wishes without undue influence or duress.

2. Appointment of Executors

2.1. I hereby nominate, constitute and appoint _____ as Executor or if this Executor is unable or unwilling to serve then I appoint _____ as alternate Executor.

2.2. I hereby give and grant the Executor all powers and authority as are required or allowed in law, and especially that of assumption.

2.3. I hereby direct that my Executors shall not be required to furnish security and shall serve without any bond.

2.4. Pending the distribution of my estate my Executors shall have authority to carry on any business, venture or partnership in which I may have any interest at the time of my death.

2.5. My Executors shall have full and absolute power in his/her discretion to insure, repair, improve or to sell all or any assets of my estate, whether by public auction or private sale and shall be entitled to let any property in my estate on such terms and conditions as will be in the best interest of my beneficiaries.

2.6. My Executors shall have authority to borrow money for any purpose connected with the liquidation and administration of my estate and to that end may encumber any of the assets of my estate.

2.7. My Executors shall have authority to engage the services of attorneys, accountants and other advisors as he/she may deem necessary to assist with the execution of this last will and testament and to pay reasonable compensation for their services from my estate.

3. Bequests

3.1. I bequeath unto the persons named below, if he or she survives me by 30 (thirty) days, the following property:

Name: _____

Relationship: _____

Address: _____

Property: _____

Name: _____

Relationship: _____

Address: _____

Property: _____

3.2. If at the time of my death any of the property described in 3.1. above is no longer in my possession or part of my estate, then the bequest of such property shall be deemed null and void and shall no longer form part of this will and testament.

3.3. If any of the persons named in 3.1. above do not survive me by 30 (thirty) days, the property bequeathed to such a person shall become part of the remainder of my estate.

3.4. If any property described above is encumbered by debt which the beneficiary of such a bequest does not want to assume liability for, such property shall revert to the remainder of my estate.

4. Remaining Property and Residual Estate

4.1. I bequeath the remainder of my estate, property and effects, whether movable or immovable, wheresoever situated and of whatsoever nature in equal shares to:

Name: _____

Relationship: _____

Address: _____

AND

Name: _____

Relationship: _____

Address: _____

4.2. If any of the beneficiaries named in 4.1. are proved to be indebted to me by means of a legal instrument, then his

/ her share of my estate shall be reduced by the amount of such debt.

4.3. Should any of the beneficiaries named in 4.1. not survive me by 30 (thirty) days I direct that the non-surviving person's share goes to his / her natural, adopted or stepchildren in equal shares.

5. Special Requests

I direct that on my death my remains shall be cremated, and all cremation expenses shall be paid out of my estate.

OR

I direct that on my death my remains shall be buried at _____ and all funeral expenses shall be paid out of my estate.

6. General

6.1. Words signifying one gender shall include the others and words signifying the singular shall include the plural and vice versa where appropriate.

6.2. Should any provision of this will be judged by an appropriate court of law as invalid it shall not affect any of the remaining provisions whatsoever.

Signed on this _____
day of _____20_____

at this location _____

in the presence of the undersigned witnesses.

SIGNED: _____

WITNESSES

As witnesses we declare that we are of sound mind and of legal age to witness a will and that to the best of our knowledge _____, the creator of this will, is of legal age to make a will, appears to be of sound mind and signed this will willingly and free of undue influence or duress. We declare that he/she signed this will in our presence as we then signed as witnesses in his / her presence and in the presence of each other witness, all being present at the same time.

Under penalty of perjury we declare these statements to be true and correct on this

_____ day of _____ 20 _____

at this location _____.

Witness 1.

Name: _____

Address: _____

Signature: _____

Witness 2.

Name: _____

Address: _____

Signature: _____

CPSIA information can be obtained
at www.ICGtesting.com
Printed in the USA
LVHW052126040121
675713LV00031B/1175